THE JEWISH LIFE CYCLE

INSTITUTE OF RELIGIOUS ICONOGRAPHY
STATE UNIVERSITY GRONINGEN

ICONOGRAPHY OF RELIGIONS

EDITED BY

TH. VAN BAAREN, L. P. VAN DEN BOSCH, H. G. KIPPENBERG, L. LEERTOUWER,
F. LEEMHUIS, H. TE VELDE, H. WITTE, AND H. BUNING (*Secretary*)

SECTION XXIII: JUDAISM

FASCICLE FOUR

LEIDEN
E. J. BRILL
1987

THE JEWISH LIFE CYCLE

BY

JOSEPH GUTMANN

Professor of Art History, Wayne State University, Detroit, Michigan

With 48 plates

LEIDEN
E. J. BRILL
1987

ISSN   169-8281
ISBN   90 04 07892 4

CONTENTS

ACKNOWLEDGEMENTS

My sincere thanks to Mr. Alfred Rubens for his gracious help in making photographs of objects in his collection available to me, and to Ms. J. Montagu, Head of the photographic collection of the Warburg Institute for her assistance. A special debt is due to Prof. Stanley F. Chyet for reading the manuscript and making many helpful suggestions for its improvement, and to Shalom Sabar for his invaluable aid.

Many of the photographs reproduced in this fascicle came from the late Prof. Franz Landsberger, Director of the Hebrew Union College Museum, who graciously bequeathed his important collection of photographs to me.

I also wish to acknowledge the help of Nancy Berman and Grace Grossman of the Hebrew Union College Skirball Museum, Iris Fishof of the Israel Museum, Bernard Fishman of the Fenster Gallery of Jewish Art, Vladimír Sadek of the State Jewish Museum, Prague, Liesel Franzheim of the Kölnisches Stadtmuseum, Prof. Dr. Otto Böcher, Prof. Dr. Freddy Raphaël, Victor Klagsbald, Michael L. Chyet, and Judith Maslin.

Grateful acknowledgment for permission to reproduce photographs in their possession is made to the authorities concerned. Sources of photographs are indicated in the explanations to the plates.

SELECTED BIBLIOGRAPHY

ALTSHULER, D., ed., *The Precious Legacy. Judaic Treasures from the Czechoslovak State Collections*. New York, 1983.

BAMBERGER, J., "Aus meiner Minhagimsammelmappe," *Jahrbuch für jüdische Volkskunde*, 1 (1923), 320-322.

BIALER, Y. L., *Jewish Life in Art and Tradition. Based on the Collection of the Sir Isaac and Lady Edith Wolfson Museum*, Hechal Shlomo, Jerusalem. New York, 1976.

BOCCATO, C., *The Ancient Jewish Cemetery of San Nicolo on the Lido in Venice*. Venice, 1980.

BODENSCHATZ, J. C. G., *Kirchliche Verfassung der heutigen Juden sonderlich derer in Deutschland*. Erlang, 1748.

CANTERA-BURGOS, F., "La '*Ketuba*' de D. Davidovitch y las ketubbot españolas," *Sefarad*, 33 (1973), 375-386.

CHILL, A., *The Minhagim: The Customs and Ceremonies of Judaism, Their Origins and Rationale*. New York, 1980².

CHRISTIANI, M. W., *Kurtze Beschreibung einer wohleingerichteten Synagog*. Regensburg, 1723.

COHEN, E. J., *Guide to Ritual Circumcision and Redemption of the First-Born Son*. New York, 1984.

CUSIN, S. G., *Art in the Jewish Tradition*. Milan, 1963.

DAN, J., "Samael, Lilith and the Concept of Evil in Early Kabbalah," *AJS Review*, 5 (1980), 17-40.

DAVIDOVITCH, D., "A Rare Parokhet for the Circumcision Ceremony," *Museum Haaretz Yearbook*, 15-16 (1974), 112-118.

——, "Die Tora-Wimpel im Braunschweigischen Landesmuseum," *Tora Wimpel: Zeugnisse jüdischer Volkskunst aus dem Braunschweigischen Landesmuseum*, ed. R. Hagan, Braunschweig, 1978, 12-27.

——, *The Ketuba. Jewish Marriage Contracts Through the Ages*. Tel-Aviv, 1968.

Detroit Institute of Arts, *Exhibition of Jewish Ceremonial Art*. Detroit, 1951.

DOLEZELOVÁ, J., "Torah Binders from Four Centuries at the State Jewish Museum in Prague," *Judaica Bohemiae*, 9 (1973), 55-71.

EHRLICH, L. E., *Die Kultsymbolik im Alten Testament und im nachbiblischen Judentum*. Stuttgart, 1959.

EIS, R., *Torah Binders from the Judah L. Magnes Museum*. Berkeley, 1979.

EISENSTEIN, J. D., *Ozar Dinim u-Minhagim*. Tel-Aviv, 1970 (Hebrew).

FIGUERAS, P., *Decorated Jewish Ossuaries*. Leiden, 1983.

FISHOF, I., " 'Jerusalem above my chief Joy': Depictions of Jerusalem in Italian Ketubot," *Journal of Jewish Art*, 9 (1982), 61-75.

FRANKEL, G., *The Art of the Jewish Paper-Cut*. Jerusalem, 1983 (Hebrew).

FRANZHEIM, L., "Hebräische Schrift — gestickt und gemalt. Tora-Wimpel des 18. und 19. Jahrhundert aus der jüdischen Abteilung des Kölnischen Stadtmuseum," *Köln und das rheinische Judentum. Festschrift Germania Judaica 1959-1984*, Cologne, 1984, 197-204.

FREEHOF, S. B., *Reform Jewish Practice and its Rabbinic Background*. Cincinnati, 1944, 2 vols.

——, "Ceremonial Creativity among the Ashkenazim," *Beauty in Holiness*, ed. Gutmann, 486-500.

——, "Home Rituals and the Spanish Synagogue," *Beauty in Holiness*, ed. Gutmann, 501-513.

——, "The Chuppah," *In the Time of Harvest*, ed. D. J. Silver, New York, 1963, 186-193.

FREEHOF, L.; B. KING, *Embroideries and Fabrics for Synagogue and Home*. New York, 1966.

FRIEDMAN, M. A., *Jewish Marriage Contracts from Palestine. A Genizah Study*. New York, 1980.

FÜRST, A., *Sitten und Gebräuche einer Judengasse*. Szekesfehervar, 1908.

GANS, M. H., *Memorbook. History of Dutch Jewry from the Renaissance to 1940*. Baarn, 1977².

GASTER, M., *The Ketubah*. New York, 1974².

GASTER, T., *The Holy and the Profane*. New York, 1955.

GOODMAN, P. and H., eds., *The Jewish Marriage Anthology*. Philadelphia, 1965.

GRASSI, L., ed., *Italian Ketubbot. Illuminated Jewish Marriage Contracts*. Milan, 1984.

GROSSMAN, C., "Womenly Arts: A Study of Italian Torah Binders in the New York Jewish Museum Collection," *Journal of Jewish Art*, 7 (1980), 35-43.

GÜDEMANN, M., *Geschichte des Erziehungswesens und der Cultur der abendländischen Juden*. Amsterdam, 1966².

GUGGENHEIM-GRÜNBERG, F., *Die Torawickelbände von Lengnau: Zeugnisse jüdischer Volkskunst*. Zürich, 1967.

GUTMANN, J., ed., *Beauty in Holiness: Studies in Jewish Customs and Ceremonial Art*. New York, 1970.

——, *Jewish Ceremonial Art*. New York, 1968².

——, "Wedding Customs and Ceremonies in Art," *Beauty in Holiness*, ed. Gutmann, 313-339.

——, *The Jewish Sanctuary*. Leiden, 1983.

——, "Christian Influences on Jewish Customs," *Spirituality and Prayer: Jewish and Christian Understandings*, eds. L. Klenicki, G. Huck. New York, 1983, 128-138.

——, "Die Mappe Schuletragen: An Unusual Judeo-German Custom," *Visible Religion*, 2 (1983), 167-173.

——, "Return in Mercy to Zion. A Messianic Dream in Jewish Art," *Land of Israel: Jewish Perspectives*, ed. L. Hoffman (in press).

HAGAN, R.; D. DAVIDOVITCH; R. BUSCH, *Tora Wimpel: Zeugnisse jüdischer Volkskunst aus dem Braunschweigischen Landesmuseum*. Braunschweig, 1978.

HALLO, R., *Schriften zur Kunstgeschichte in Kassel. Sammlungen, Denkmäler, Judaica*, ed. G. Schweikhart. Kassel, 1983.

Hebrew Union College Skirball Museum, *A Walk through the Past*, ed. N. Berman. Los Angeles, 1974.

HEŘMAN, J., *Jewish Cemeteries in Bohemia and Moravia*. Prague, n.d.

HINTZE, E., *Katalog der ... Ausstellung. Das Judentum in der Geschichte Schlesiens*. Breslau, 1929.

Historia Hebraica, *Ausstellungs-Katalog des Staatlichen Jüdischen Museums Prag in Zusammenarbeit mit der Jüdische Gemeinde zu Berlin*, ed. I. Pruschnowski. Berlin, 1965.

Historisches Museum Frankfurt am Main, *Synagoga. Jüdische Altertümer, Handschriften und Kultgeräte*. Frankfurt/Main, 1961.

ISAAC, E., "The Enigma of Circumcision," *Commentary* (January, 1967), 52-55.

Israel Museum Jerusalem, *Jewish Treasures from Paris: From the Collections of the Cluny Museum and the Consistoire*, ed. V. A. Klagsbald. Jerusalem, 1980.

——, *Moritz Oppenheim: The First Jewish Painter*, ed. E. Cohen. Jerusalem, 1983.

——, *Jewish Tradition in Art: The Feuchtwanger Collection of Judaica*, ed. I. Shachar; tr. R. Grafman. Jerusalem, 1981.

Jewish Art Treasures in Venice, ed. G. Reinisch Sullam. New York, n.d.

Jewish Art Treasures from Prague, *The State Jewish Museum in Prague and its Collection*. Catalog of Exhibition at Whitworth Art Gallery, ed. C. R. Dodwell. London-Manchester, 1980.

Jewish Historical Museum Amsterdam, *Joods Historisch Museum*, ed. J. C. E. Belinfante. Haarlem, 1978.

Jewish Community in Rome, *Permanent Exhibition Catalogue*. Rome, n.d.

Jewish Museum London, *Catalogue of the Permanent and Loan Collections of the Jewish Museum London*, ed. R. D. Barnett. London, 1974.

Jewish Museum New York, *Danzig 1939: Treasures of a Destroyed Community*, eds. V. Mann, J. Gutmann. New York-Detroit, 1980.

——, *Fabric of Jewish Life: Textiles from the Jewish Museum Collection*, eds. B. Kirshenblatt-Gimblett, C. Grossman. New York, 1977.

——, *Kings and Citizens: The History of the Jews in Denmark 1622-1983*. New York, 1983.

——, *A Tale of Two Cities: Jewish Life in Frankfurt and Istanbul 1750-1870*, ed. V. Mann. New York, 1982.

Judaica, *Die Sammlung Berger*, eds. M. Berger, W. Häusler, E. Lessing. Munich, 1979.

KANOF, A., *Jewish Ceremonial Art and Religious Observance*. New York, 1970.

KASHANI, R., *Illustrated Ketubot of Afghanistan*. Jerusalem, 1979 (Hebrew).

KATZ, K., P. P. KAHANE, M. BROSHI, *From the Beginning. Archaeology and Art in the Israel Museum Jerusalem*. London, 1968.

KAYSER, S. S., G. SCHOENBERGER, *Jewish Ceremonial Art*. Philadelphia, 1959^2.

KIRCHNER, P. C., *Jüdisches Ceremoniel*. Nürnberg, 1724.

KIRSHENBLATT-GIMBLETT, B., "The Cut that Binds. The Western Ashkenazic Torah Binder as Nexus between Circumcision and Torah," *Celebration. Studies in Festivity and Ritual*, ed. V. Turner, Washington, D.C., 1982, 136-146.

KLEEBLATT, N., G. WERTKIN, *The Jewish Heritage in American Folk Art*. New York, 1984.

Kölnisches Stadtmuseum, *Judaica*, ed. L. Franzheim. Cologne, 1980.

KRAJEWSKA, M., *Time of Stones*. Warsaw, 1983.

KRAUSS, S., *Synagogale Altertümer*. Berlin-Vienna, 1922.

KRAUTHEIMER, R., *Mittelalterliche Synagogen*. Berlin, 1927.

KRÜGER, R., *Die Kunst der Synagoge. Eine Einführung in die Probleme von Kunst und Kult des Judentums*. Leipzig, 1966.

LANDSBERGER, F., "Illuminated Marriage Contracts," *Beauty in Holiness*, ed. Gutmann, 370-413.

——, *Einführung in die jüdische Kunst*. Berlin, 1935.

LAUTERBACH, J. Z., "The Ceremony of Breaking a Glass at Weddings," *Beauty in Holiness*, ed. Gutmann, 340-369.

LAZAR, H., "Jonah, the Tower, and the Lions: An Eighteenth-Century Italian Silver Book Binding," *Journal of Jewish Art*, 3/4 (1977), 58-73.

——, "A propos d'une *ketubah* italienne du XVIIe siècle: Réemploi de support et épithalame," *Revue des études juives*, 138 (1979), 367-383.

LEON, H. J., *The Jews of Ancient Rome*. Philadelphia, 1960.

Levinson, P. N., *Kultsymbolik im Alten Testament und im nachbiblischen Judentum*. Stuttgart, 1972 (Illustrations to the book by Ehrlich).

Lion, J., *The Old Prague Jewish Cemetery*. Prague, 1960.

Löw, L., *Die Lebensalter in der jüdischen Literatur*. Szegedin, 1875.

Margaritha, A., *Der gantze jüdische Glaube*. Leipzig, 1705.

Matts, A., *Reasons for Jewish Customs and Traditions*. New York, 1968.

Maurice Spertus Museum of Judaica Chicago, *An Illustrated Catalog of Selected Objects*, eds. A. Feldman, G. C. Grossman. Chicago, 1974.

——, *Magic and Superstition in the Jewish Tradition*, ed. M. R. Josephy. Chicago, 1975.

Mazar, B., N. Avigad, *Beth She'arim*, I, III. New Brunswick, N.J., 1973, 1976.

Metzger, T. and M., *Jewish Life in the Middle Ages. Illuminated Hebrew Manuscripts from the Thirteenth to the Sixteenth Centuries*. New York, 1982.

Mielziner, M., *The Jewish Law of Marriage and Divorce in Ancient and Modern Times*. Cincinnati, 1884.

Mishkan Le'omanut, *Museum of Art, Ein Harod*, ed. Z. Efron. Ein Harod, 1970.

Mitteilungen der Gesellschaft zur Erforschung jüdischer Kunstdenkmäler zu Frankfurt am Main, I-X. Düsseldorf-Frankfurt/Main, 1900-1927.

Morgenstern, J., *Rites of Birth, Marriage, Death and Kindred Occasions among the Semites*. Cincinnati, 1960.

Moses, E., *Jüdische Kult- und Kunstdenkmäler. Aus der Geschichte der Juden im Rheinland*. Düsseldorf, 1931.

Muneles, O., *Prague Ghetto in the Renaissance Period*. Prague, 1965.

Musée Juif de Suisse à Bâle, *L'année juive*, ed. N. Rosenan. Zürich, 1976.

Negarestan Museum Teheran, *Iranian Wedding Contracts of the Nineteenth and Twentieth Centuries*, ed. L. Soudavar Diba. Teheran, 1976 (Persian and English).

Picart, B., *The Ceremonies and Religious Customs of the Various Nations of the Known World*. London, 1733.

Pollack, H., *Jewish Folkways in Germanic Lands (1648-1806)*. Cambridge, Mass., 1971.

Reuter, F., *WARMAISA. 1000 Jahre Juden in Worms*. Worms, 1984.

Roth, C., ed., *Jewish Art: An Illustrated History*. Greenwich, Ct., 1971, rev. ed. B. Narkiss.

Roth, E., ed., *Festschrift zur Wiedereinweihung der Alten Synagoge zu Worms*. Frankfurt/Main, 1961.

Royal Albert Hall London, *Catalogue of Anglo-Jewish Historical Exhibition, 1887*. London, 1887.

Rubens, A., *A Jewish Iconography*. London, 1981, rev. ed.

Sabar, S., "The Use and Meaning of Christian Motifs in Illustrations of Jewish Wedding Contracts in Italy," *Journal of Jewish Art*, 10 (1984), 47-63.

——, "The Beginnings and Flourishing of Ketubbah Illustration in Italy: A Study in Popular Imagery and Jewish Patronage during the 17th and 18th Centuries," Unpublished Ph.D. dissertation, University of California, Los Angeles, California (in progress).

Schauss, H., *The Lifetime of a Jew throughout the Ages of Jewish History*. Cincinnati, 1950.

Scheiber, A., *Jewish Inscriptions in Hungary*. Leiden, 1983.

Scheyer, E., "The Iconography of Jacob van Ruisdael's Cemetery," *Bulletin of the Detroit Institute of Arts*, 55 (1977), 133-146.

Schnitzler, O., "Jüdische Beschneidungsamulette aus Süddeutschland, dem Elsass, der Schweiz und aus Hessen," *Schweizerisches Archiv für Volkskunde*, 74 (1978), 41-45.

Schrire, T., *Hebrew Amulets: Their Decipherment and Interpretation*. London, 1966.

Schubert, K., K. Lohrmann, eds., *1000 Jahre Österreichisches Judentum*. Eisenstadt, 1982.

Seidman, G., "Marriage Rings Jewish Style," *Connoisseur*, 206 (1981), 48-51.

Shachar, I., " 'Feast and Rejoice in Brotherly Love': Burial Society Glasses and Jugs from Bohemia and Moravia," *The Israel Museum News*, 9 (1972), 22-51.

Stadtmuseum Köln, *Monumenta Judaica. 2000 Jahre Geschichte und Kultur am Rhein*, ed. K. Schilling. Cologne, 1964.

Städtisches Museum Göttingen, *700 Jahre Juden in Niedersachsen. Geschichte und religiöses Leben*. Göttingen, 1973.

Stillman, Y. K., "The Middle Eastern Amulet as Folk Art," *Studies in Aggadah and Jewish Folklore*, eds. I. Ben-Ami, J. Dan, Jerusalem, 1983, 95-101.

Ungerleider Mayerson, J., *Folk Art in the Jewish Tradition*. New York (in press).

Van Der Zwan, P. J. Abbink, "Ornamentation on Eighteenth-Century Torah Binders," *The Israel Museum News*, 14 (1978), 65-73.

Vega, L. A., *The Beth Haim of Ouderkerk aan de Amstel: Images of a Portuguese Jewish Cemetery in Holland*. Amsterdam, 1975.

Ward, J., *Rings through the Ages*. New York, 1981.

Weinstein, R., "A Stone of Remembrance," *Journal of Jewish Art*, 1 (1974), 66-79.

——, "Sepulchral Monuments of the Jews of Amsterdam in the Seventeenth and Eighteenth Centuries," Unpublished Ph.D. dissertation, New York University, 1979.

WEISS, C., "Motives for Male Circumcision among Preliterate and Literate Peoples," *Journal of Sex Research*, 2 (1966), 69-88.

WERNER, A., *Pictures of Traditional Jewish Family Life by Moritz Daniel Oppenheim*. New York, 1976.

WEYL, R., F. RAPHAEL, *L'imagerie juive d'Alsace*. Strasbourg, 1979.

WEYL, R. and M., "Mappot d'Alsace," *Saisons d'Alsace*, 20 (1975), 119-133.

WILSON, W. H., " 'The Circumcision,' A Drawing by Romeyn de Hooghe," *Master Drawings*, 13 (1975), 250-258.

WOLFF, L., *Universal-Agende für jüdische Kultusbeamte*. Berlin, 1891².

Yeshiva University Museum New York, *The Jewish Wedding*, ed. S. Pappenheim. New York, 1977.

ZIMMELS, H. J., *Ashkenazim and Sephardim. Their Relations, Differences, and Problems as Reflected in the Rabbinical Responsa*. London, 1958.

INTRODUCTION

Central to classical Jewish religion is the daily performance of *mitzvot*, divinely ordained deeds or acts. In complying with a *mitzvah*, a Jew blesses and prays to God "who has sanctified us by His *mitzvot* and commanded us [to observe them]." Rabbinic tradition speaks of both the *hibbuv mitzvah*, ardent devotion to the fulfillment of religious commandments, and the *hiddur mitzvah*, beautification of the commandments. The rabbis derived the concept of *hiddur mitzvah* from the verse in Exodus 15:2: "This is my God and I will beautify [literally, enshrine or glorify] Him." Hence, Judaism stresses both the affective and the aesthetic functions of the *mitzvot*—the emotion involved in carrying out the *mitzvah* and the edification inspired by *mitzvot* through the use of splendid ceremonial objects so that Jewish worshippers can be holy before God, while God can be worshipped in the "beauty of holiness." The obligation to carry out *mitzvot* sets Judaism apart from Christianity where the emphasis tends to be credal, stressing belief rather than deeds or acts. Furthermore, the demand to endow with the greatest beauty every object used in religious ceremonies underscores signal differences between Judaism and Christianity.

In Christian worship the objects used in the sacraments are considered sacred as they serve to help invoke the redeeming power of the actual divine presence, whereas in Judaism the sacramental aspect is absent and the predominant function of objects used in the life cycle ceremonies is to enhance the worship of the invisible Deity. The Jewish objects are not sacred in themselves; they are a means to help approach Divinity, but never the means through which the Divine becomes manifest.

Although Judaism with its discipline is one of the oldest surviving religions of mankind, it is at the same time a dynamic religion reflecting a unique involvement with many diverse civilizations. Thus the ceremonial objects used and the very ceremonial acts connected with them in the life cycle refract constant innovation and change as Judaism has encountered new societies and cultures in its long passage through history. The ceremonies and objects cannot be separated from the larger context of which Judaism is an integral part. Hence, the customs and the ceremonial objects employed in Jewish life cycle observances are inseparably connected with objects and customs of Ancient Western Asia and the Hellenistic, Roman, Parthian, Sasanian, Muslim and Christian worlds.

It is this very involvement in the larger cultural context that demanded constant and major alteration not only in the art forms employed, but in the very ceremonies themselves. It should not be surprising, therefore, that the unity of practice frequently stressed in popular books on the customs, ceremonies and art objects of Judaism is imaginary and that the reality is one of a rich diversity varying from country to country and from century to century. This encounter with new cultures and civilizations has not only engendered a complex variegation in Jewish customs and artforms, but also considerable divisiveness.

No better evidence can be brought than the *Arba'ah Turim*, the law code of the *Ashkenazi* (German) scholar Jacob ben Asher. Written in fourteenth-century Spain, it proved unacceptable to the *Sefardim* (established Spanish Jews), because Jacob ben Asher frequently chose to include only Ashkenazi practices. In the same way the *Shulḥan Arukh*, the law code of the sixteenth-century Sefardi compiler Joseph Caro, was unacceptable to many Jews in northern Europe as the author neglected Ashkenazi customs. How divisive life cycle ceremonies and their ceremonial objects can be is underscored by the caution Isaac de Pinto, a Sefardi Jew living in eighteenth-century Holland, addressed to Voltaire:

> Mr. Voltaire cannot be ignorant of the scrupulous exactness of the Portuguese and Spanish Jews [the Sefardim] not to intermix in marriage alliance, or any other way, with the Jews of other nations [i.e., with Ashkenazi Jews]. He has been to Holland and knows they have separate synagogues, and that, although they profess the same religion and the same articles of faith, yet their ceremonies have often no resemblance. The manners of the Portuguese [i.e., Sefardi] Jews are also very different from those of the rest; the former have no beards nor any thing peculiar in their dress. The rich among them vie with the other nations of [Western] Europe in refinement, elegance and show, and differ from them in worship only. Their variance with their other brethren is at such a height, that if a Portuguese Jew in England or Holland married a German Jewess, he would of course lose all his prerogatives, be no longer reckoned a member of their synagogue, forfeit all civil and ecclesiastical preferments, be absolutely divorced from the body of the nation, and not even be buried with his Portuguese brethren.[1]

Similarly, the twelfth-century Spanish Jewish scholar Abraham bar Ḥiyyah mocked the recently introduced Ashkenazi practice of reciting a mourner's *kaddish*: "Anyone who believes that after his death he can be benefited by the actions of his sons and their prayers for him is harboring false ideas [i.e., self-delusion]."[2]

In Germany itself, the twelfth-thirteenth century Judah ben Samuel (called *he-Ḥasid*, the Pietist) lamented that "Jewish customs (*minhagim*) in many places [within Germany] are like those practiced by non-Jews [i.e., Christians]."[3]

Yet notwithstanding the diversity of Jewish ceremonial styles and the talmudic exhortation to fashion beautiful ritual objects, no cult objects used in life cycle ceremonies in biblical times have come down to us nor do we have tangible artistic evidence of life cycle objects used in the talmudic period or even the Middle Ages. How are we to account for this lack of life cycle objects for one of the oldest surviving religions of mankind? The answer is two-fold.

In the first place, most of the ceremonial objects that are taken for granted today in life cycle ceremonies apparently did not come into being until the Middle Ages. Secondly, the continual forced migrations suffered by Jews in many medieval communities were responsible for objects being lost, stolen, destroyed and melted down. Thus the history of the surviving ceremonial objects unfolds during the last half-millenium in various communities of Christian and Islamic society. The stress of this study will be laid on the life cycle ceremonies and objects used by Jews in Christian Europe in the last 500 years, as some of these have been examined by scholars. The Jewish objects and ceremonies used in the Islamic world have still to be systematically studied.

---

[1] J. Gutmann, "Prolegomenon," *Beauty in Holiness: Studies in Jewish Customs and Ceremonial Art* (New York, 1970), IX-X.

[2] J. Gutmann, "Christian Influences on Jewish Customs," *Spirituality and Prayer: Jewish and Christian Understandings*, eds. L. Klenicki and G. Huck (New York, 1983), 128.

[3] *Ibid.*, 138, n. 31.

Objects employed for life cycle ceremonies are developed sometimes for purely aesthetic reasons, sometimes to answer practical needs. At times appurtenances were introduced by the rabbis for polemic reasons; occasionally they were absorbed from the general—non-Jewish—environment and only gradually acquired a religious sanctity.

It should also be noted that the interests of the Church and the Christian guild system in medieval Western Europe generally forced Jews to support themselves as moneylenders and petty tradesmen. Excluded from Christian guilds Jews in the West were virtually forced to have life cycle ceremonial objects made by leading Christian craftsmen. In Eastern Europe, however, and especially Poland, the absence of a middle class and of strong guilds led to the encouragement and promotion of Jewish craftsmen and the formation of Jewish guilds. Hence, many Jewish ceremonial objects were made by Jews residing in Poland.

I. Birth

1. *Berit Milah* (Circumcision)

One of the greatest *mitzvot* (commandments) in classical Judaism is to bring children, and especially boys, into the world. The stress on male children in Judaism hardly differs from that of other religions, for it was not until the twentieth century that women could assert any sort of equality in Western society. Celibacy, so widely practiced in many other ancient religions, never took firm root in Judaism. Religious observances in Judaism were primarily written by, for and of men. Women in Judaism until recent times were valued largely because they performed the vital function of giving birth to children and rearing them within a male-dominated society. It is primarily the male who is deemed to stand in a covenantal relationship with God and it is the male alone who can initiate significant *mitzvot* that have binding covenantal implications.

The first important covenantal relationship of the Jewish male child begins at the *berit milah* (covenant of circumcision) usually performed on the eighth day after birth, sometimes by the father in biblical times (Genesis 21:4) and subsequently from the talmudic period on by a specially trained *mohel* (circumciser), who may or may not be the child's father. The Babylonian Talmud (*Nedarim* 32a) exclaims that "exalted is circumcision, for it outweighs all the [other] *mitzvot* of the Torah." So sacred is this first covenant that it can be performed on the Sabbath and even on the holiest day of the Jewish year, *Yom Kippur*. Even if a Jewish child dies before the eighth day, rabbinic law requires circumcision before burial.

The child is nameless until the eighth day. It is only when the son is symbolically bound to the covenant of Abraham that he receives his Hebrew name.

The motives for the adoption of circumcision have often been explored by scholars in such disciplines as Bible, comparative religion, psychology, medicine and anthropology. No consensus of opinion has emerged among scholars and the origins of the rite remain obscure. The practice of circumcision in literate and non-literate societies, outside of Judaism, has been explained as a *rite de passage*, an initiation rite symbolically marking the boy's death and resurrection and his acceptance as a responsible full member of the community. Some scholars feel that circumcision was a substitute for castration or human sacrifice—a *pars pro toto* rite or that it served as a distinct tribal mark, a sign of "ethnic" identification. Other scholars assert that it was done for hygienic or medical reasons. Circumcision has also been associated with marriage or fertility rites.

Jewish tradition attributes the rite to the biblical Abraham, who at age 99 circumcised himself and his entire household: "You shall circumcise the flesh of your foreskin and that shall be a sign of the covenant between Me and you. At the age of eight days, every male among you throughout the generations shall be circumcised" (Genesis 17:10ff.). The critical approach to the Bible, however, assigns the practice of circumcision on the eighth day to the Priestly Code of the fifth-fourth century B.C.E. As such the rite of circumcision on the eighth day cannot belong to the time of Abraham, but is a projection by the priestly writers of later practices back into the semi-nomadic period of Abraham (cf. Leviticus 12:3). The relevant biblical passages give few clues as to the real origin and purpose of circumcision in ancient Israel. As in other societies, it may originally have been a *rite de passage*, a rite of initiation, which the priestly writers transformed into a covenantal commitment of purification, dedication and identification. This rite was not exclusive to Judaism, but was known in ancient Egypt and was practiced in Edom, Moab, Ammon and among Arabs (Jeremiah 9:25).

Originally in biblical times *berit milah* may simply have consisted of cutting the ᶜ*orlah* (foreskin) with a flint knife (Exodus 4:25 and Joshua 5:2). The rabbis of the talmudic period perhaps added *periᶜah* (the tearing of the genital mucous membrane and laying bare the glans), and *metzitzah*, when the *mohel* fills his mouth with wine and applies suction either orally or through a mouthpiece to stanch the flow of blood (Babylonian Talmud, *Shabbat* 133a-b) (Plate XIa). This latter practice has now been generally abandoned. During the talmudic period, the circumcision was normally held at home, but was shifted to the synagogue during the geonic period.

Especially in the Ashkenazi (Franco-German) region, it was deemed necessary to protect the child and mother from spirits and demons such as Lilith, who, popular belief held, had power to harm or kill mother and child (Plate I). Lilith's history is complex. She is mentioned in ancient Western Asian sources. She gains popularity through a late geonic work known as the *Alfa Beta of Ben Sira* (or *Pseudo-Ben Sira*). According to *Pseudo-Ben Sira*, she was created equal to Adam and was his first wife. However, as Lilith and Adam constantly quarreled, she pronounced the Holy Name of God, flew into the air and thus fled from Adam. Adam immediately pleaded for her return and God dispatched three angels to fetch her. The angels found her somewhere near the Red Sea. When she refused to return, even by force and under threats, the three angels struck a bargain with her. They made Lilith swear by God's Name that whenever she saw them or their names—Sanoi, Sansanoi and Semangalof—on an amulet, she would not harm that child. Furthermore, her power to harm male babies extended only to the eighth day, though for females somewhat longer.[4]

In order to safeguard against Lilith and other demons, tablets, talismans and amulets were hung on the child and around the room of the woman in confinement. Tablets (called *Kindbett-Tafeln*, -*Briefchen* or -*Zettel*; *Kimpetzetl* in Poland) generally date from the eighteenth century on and took various shapes and forms in different European areas. Often they

---

[4] J. Dan, "Samael, Lilith and the Concept of Evil in Early Kabbalah," *AJS Review*, 5 (1980), 17-40.

carried incantations against Lilith and her evil horde. The formula on the wall tablets or in a magic circle inscribed on the floor frequently read: "Almighty, rend Satan; Adam and Eve—barring Lilith; Sanoi, Sansanoi, Semangalof" (Plates IIa-b, IIIa).

In Italy amulets made of precious metal were placed in the baby's cradle. They were called *Shaddai* (Almighty) because they carried the word *Shaddai* and such Jewish symbols as the *menorah* (Plate IIIc).

The most dangerous time of all was the night before circumcision as it was believed demons and evil spirits would make a final concerted effort to attack mother and child. Popular belief held that the power of these evil forces (called *shedim* and *mazikim*) would be broken only after circumcision. Hence a night vigil was instituted. This medieval Jewish vigil was called *Wachnacht* (*Wachtnacht* or *leil shimurim*). Men and women gathered in the home of the woman in childbed. They lit candles, recited prayers, and studied (*lernen*) selections from Psalms, the Talmud and the Zohar throughout the night (Plate I). At times the circumcision knife was placed under the pillow of the woman in confinement or a sword or knife was suspended from the bed (Plate IIIb). Iron, it was believed, frightened evil spirits.

Three days before the circumcision ceremony it became customary, especially in the Rhineland, to summon women friends and relatives to the home of the woman in child-bed. The *shammash* (a synagogal functionary) called out in the streets: "Zu der Judsch Kerz" (= *Jüdischkerze*, to the circumcision candle). When assembled in the home, the women often made one large candle with twelve intertwined strands of wax or twelve small wax candles and one large candle. The twelve strands or small candles symbolized the twelve tribes of Israel and the large candle was called *ner tamid* (eternal light). No illustration of this custom has come down to us, and this Ashkenazi ceremony, like some others, is no longer observed.

On the day of the circumcision, the boy, wearing special garments (Plate IVb), was brought to a particular door of the synagogue, known as *Judsch Tirchen* (= *Jüdisch-Tür*, circumcision door), sometimes by a woman, called *sandeket*, *sandakit* or *Gevatterin* (Plate IVa). As women could not enter the synagogue proper, but were confined to a separate room adjoining the main synagogue or were assigned a separate area, often a balcony, the child was handed to a godfather (called *sandak*, *sandek*, *sandik* or *baal berit*). Sometimes the god-father was called *Gevatter* in Germany (*Kvater* in Poland). At other times the *Gevatter* simply assisted the *sandak* by holding the boy's legs.

Ceremonies like *Wachnacht*, the wax candles, special garments, and the circumcision door were adopted from Christians, among whom, of course, such rituals were linked to Baptism.[5]

In Christianity, too, it was the *synteknos* or *syndikos* (the word *sandak* may be derived from it), who acted as godfather and lifted the neophyte from the baptismal waters. The god-father, whether called *sandak* or *Gevatter*, had the function of holding the child on his knees during circumcision. In addition, a special chair, known as the Chair or Throne of Elijah (*kiss'e Eliyahu*), is first attested to in the eighth-ninth-century work, *Pirkei de Rabbi Eliezer* 29. At times, the *sandak* sat on a specially carved chair, but the preference in Ashkenazi regions was for a bench with two seats. Most of the surviving examples date from the

---

[5] Gutmann, "Christian Influences on Jewish Customs," 130-131.

eighteenth century on (Plates V-VII). Often the child was placed on Elijah's right seat by the *mohel* and then on the bench or chair reserved for the *sandak*. These seats frequently had beautiful decorative cushions or covers and the *sandak* placed the circumcision cushion on his knees while he held the child (Plates IVa, VIIIa-b).

The biblical prophet Elijah was considered the guardian angel of the covenant. Tradition linked Elijah's presence at every Jewish boy's circumcision with two biblical passages: Malachi 3:1, which refers to "the angel of the covenant," and I Kings 19:1, which praises Elijah as "moved by zeal for the Lord, the God of Hosts, for the Israelites have forsaken Your covenant." Because Elijah is the angel or guardian of the covenant and in remembrance of his zeal in upholding the covenant during the hostile regime of Ahab and Jezebel, he is welcomed at the beginning of the circumcision ceremony with the following words (at times carved on the Chair of Elijah): "This is the Chair of Elijah, may he be remembered for good."

In prayers uttered by the father and the *mohel*, the fervent hope is expressed that the act of circumcision may be equated with an actual sacrificial offering and accredited to the participants in the circumcision ceremony as if they had sacrificed the child on God's altar just as Abraham was prepared to do with Isaac. Special oval plates from nineteenth-century Galicia are found in many collections which carry the scene of the Binding of Isaac (*Akedat Yitzḥak*, Plate XVIIa). These plates have been variously linked with the Circumcision or the *Pidyon ha-ben* (Redemption of the first-born son) ceremony. As the *Akedat Yitzḥak* has been associated with the circumcision ceremony rather than with the redemption of the first-born, the plates may have been used during that ceremony.

The circumcision instruments (Plates IX-Xa-b) consisted of a forskin shield, silver wine cups (Plate XIa), a sharp double-edged circumcision knife (Plate XIb-d), a padded ring on which to seat the baby after circumcision, cotton and a phial for oil, astringent powder to promote healing and a vessel containing sand for the ʿorlah (foreskin). We also read of a small pit filled with sand underneath the large *Ḥanukkah menorah*, where the foreskins were buried.[6]

Several circumcision Torah curtains, dating from the eighteenth century on, have survived. Some of these have the service of the circumcision embroidered on them.[7] Illustrated circumcision books (*mohel* books) listing the circumcisions performed, the prayers of the circumcision rite, grace after meals, etc., also abound.

When the circumcision is over the father utters the following prayer: "Praised be You, O Lord our God, King of the universe, who has sanctified us with His *mitzvot* and has commanded us to initiate [this boy] into the covenant of Abraham, our father." Those assembled then respond: "As he has been initiated into the covenant [of Abraham], so may he be introduced to [the study of] Torah, get married [*ḥuppah*] and [perform] good deeds" (Babylonian Talmud, *Shabbat* 137b). This last pious sentiment is also embroidered on Torah binders.

2. *Die Mappe Schuletragen* (Carrying the *Wimpel* to the Synagogue)

Embroidered Torah binders were especially popular among German Jewry. It became customary to take the swaddling cloth upon which the boy had been circumcised, wash it,

[6] J. Gutmann, *The Jewish Sanctuary* (Leiden, 1983), 14.
[7] *Ibid.*, 13.

cut it generally into four sections, stitch them together and embroider them in order to make a Torah binder. The standard formula on the binder (variously called *Wimpel, Wimple* or *Mappe*) was: ''...(Hebrew name of the child), son of ... (Hebrew name of the father), may he live long and happily (or, may His rock—i.e., God—guard him and keep him in life), born under a good constellation (*mazzal tov*, the constellation corresponding to the month the child was born) on (day of the week, Hebrew date, month and year), may he grow (or may the Lord cause him to grow, or may the Lord make him worthy to grow) to [the study of] *Torah*, to get married (*huppah*), and to [perform] good deeds. Amen, Selah.''

The *Wimpel* may vary in length from around two to four meters. Many of these Torah binders utilized linen, but richer families also used silk, which gave rise to such popular sayings as ''on the birth of 'so and so's' child you could hear the silk rustle.'' Often the extant seventeenth-century examples carry no figural decoration. Prior to the eighteenth century the *Wimpel* was embroidered, but by that time the Hebrew letters were frequently painted on by Torah scribes. Patterns or stencils were also employed. In the eighteenth century it became customary to insert the boy's secular name (*hamkhuneh* = called) after his Hebrew name. It also became common to have next to the words *mazzal tov* a depiction of the constellation under which the child was born (e.g., at times a lion, the sign for Leo, ʾaryeh, will be shown for the months of *Tammuz-Av*); next to the word *Torah*, a man or boy would hold up or read from the pentateuchal scroll; and near the word *huppah* would appear a couple underneath a portable canopy whose four poles are at times held aloft by four youths (Plates XII-XIII).

The custom probably originated in Bavaria around 1500, although none of the many surviving examples date earlier than the mid-seventeenth century. The lettering used on the *Wimpel* was the square Ashkenazi script, while the letters themselves were filled with floral, animal, and bird motifs as well as human figures. These whimsical letters are familiar to us from fourteenth-fifteenth-century German Gothic Hebrew manuscripts. Some of the additional ornamentations follow those found on contemporary Christian peasant embroideries and handwritten baptismal certificates.

When the *Wimpel* was not in use it was kept in a box or chest. A ritually unfit *Wimpel* (*pasul*—torn or mutilated) was buried in the Jewish cemetery or was kept in the synagogue's *genizah* (or *Schemeskastl*, a hiding or storage place designated for this purpose). When the boy became *Bar Mitzvah*, it was customary to use his *Wimpel* to bind the Torah scroll from which he read. It was considered a *mitzvah* for a virgin or bride to embroider the *Wimpel*. On *Simhat Torah* eve in seventeenth-century Worms, the privilege (*mitzvah*) to roll up the loose Wimpels that had adorned Torah scrolls was auctioned off to women. Until 1876 when a birth registry was officially introduced in Germany, the synagogue *Wimpel* served that function.

The presentation of the *Wimpel* took place in the synagogue, usually at Sabbath morning services, but the time of presentation varied from one month to five years in different communities (Plate XIV).[8]

German Catholics reportedly had baptismal swaddling cloths embroidered with pious sentiments, and possibly this is what inspired the *Wimpel* custom. The Ashkenazi custom,

---

[8] J. Gutmann, ''Die Mappe Schuletragen: An Unusual Judeo-German Custom,'' *Visible Religion*, 2 (1983), 167-173.

which may have begun in Bavaria, rapidly spread to other German regions and to neighboring countries such as Bohemia, Moravia, Alsace, Switzerland and Denmark. It is worth noting that the *Wimpel* did not take root in Ashkenazi Poland, although Polish Jewry originated largely in medieval Germany. Apparently, at the time of their flight from the German lands, this custom had not yet been firmly established.

II. *Hollekreisch*

In Southern Germany, and especially in Bavaria, we find the emergence of another interesting custom, called *Hollekreisch* (or *Holegrasch* or *shem ha-ʿarisah* = cradle name). It may have emerged in the fourteenth century and is illustrated in one sixteenth-century manuscript (Plate XVa-b). We note on the right the mother preparing refreshments and on the left two men lifting the child in the cradle. It became customary to hold this ceremony in the parents' home on the fourth Sabbath after the birth of the child. This would occur after Sabbath morning services, which the mother attended for the first time following her confinement. Usually the invited children encircled the cradle—boys in case of a male child and girls in case of a female birth. The purpose of the gathering was to give the child a secular name. In the case of a boy, of course, a Hebrew name had already been bestowed at the circumcision ceremony. After introductory prayers taken from Scripture, such as Genesis 1:1ff. and 48:16, the children lifted the cradle three times, or sometimes the cantor (*ḥazzan*) lifted the cradle, while they called out "*Hollekreisch, Hollekreisch*, what shall we name the child?" In some communities, it was customary to place a *tallit* and Pentateuch (*ḥumash*) in the cradle. The name *Hollekreisch* for this curious ceremony has been explained as stemming from Hebrew (*ḥol karaʾ*, i.e., to shout or call out the non-Hebrew name) and from French (*haler* or *haut la crèche* = lift up or raise the cradle), or as related to Frau Holle (or Hulda, Holda), a witch who attacks infants. If the latter interpretation is valid, the name *Hollekreisch* may simply mean to encircle (*kreisen*) or call off (*kreischen*) Dame Holle before she injures the child.

III. *Pidyon ha-ben* (Redemption of the First-Born Son)

While the *Hollekreisch* ceremony was restricted primarily to Germany, the *pidyon ha-ben*, was universally observed by Jews. As every first born son who breached the mother's womb belonged to God, a father was in duty bound to redeem him from a *kohen* (priest) so that the son might be relieved of priestly duties in the Sanctuary (cf. Exodus 13:2, 13; 22:28, 34:20 and Numbers 3:12-13, 40ff.; 8:16-18). Only Levites and priests already consecrated to the service of God were exempt from this rite, which survived even the destruction of the Jerusalem Temple when the function of the priesthood, the intermediaries between God and man, ceased. Every father was still obligated on the 31st day after the boy's birth to symbolically redeem him from a *kohen* (a descendent of the Temple priesthood). In an Aramaic dialogue the priest asks the father if he wishes to deliver the son for priestly service or to redeem him for five shekels (or *selʿaim* or the equivalent in the currency of the country where the ceremony took place; the State of Israel has now minted special *shekel* coins which can be used for this ceremony) (Plate XVIa-b).

After the priest accepts the symbolic offering, the ceremony concludes with the *kohen* placing his hands upon the infant's head and pronouncing the three-fold priestly blessing.

Special plates, mostly dating from the eighteenth century on, were fashioned for the *pidyon ha-ben* ceremony. At times the child was brought in on one large plate and a smaller plate was reserved for the five shekel offering. Occasionally the metal plates might be decorated with a child in swaddling cloths and with the two hands outspread over his head, to symbolize the priestly benediction.

If for some reason the child could not be redeemed on the thirty-first day, as the father had died or was prevented from carrying out the ritual, a metal medallion was suspended around the child's neck. Written on this medallion were the words *ben kohen* (son of a priest, or belonging to the priest) or simply the Hebrew letter *he*, which stood for the five shekels (or *sel'aim*). These medallions served as a reminder that it was the child's duty to redeem himself at maturity (usually considered to be at age thirteen) (Plate XVIIb).

IV. Initiation into the Instruction of Torah

Study of Torah was an important event in the Jewish child's life. Attendance at a Jewish school was mandatory at around age five. The boy's initiation to Torah study was celebrated in the Middle Ages on the late spring *Shavuot* holiday, commemorating the day on which the Torah was given to Israel.

An early fourteenth-century South German *maḥzor* depicts in the center of the marginal illustration a child wrapped in the cloak of the father or that of a pious and learned Jew to protect him against the evil eye (Plate XVIII). The child, who is being brought to the synagogue or house of the teacher, holds in his hand a honey cake and an egg. To the left the teacher wearing his *Judenhut* (Jew's hat), is seated on a schoolbench and is taking each child on his lap. The teacher then hands the child a slate on which the Hebrew alphabet, the verse "when Moses charged us with [the study of] Torah as the heritage of the congregation of Jacob" (Deuteronomy 33:4) and the beginning verses of the book of Leviticus are written. As the teacher reads the words and letters on the slate, the pupil repeats them. Then honey is spread on the slate which the child licks off. The honey cake and an egg also had scriptural lessons on them (such as Isaiah 50:4-5 and Ezekiel 3:3) which the teacher read and the child repeated. The conclusion of the ceremony called for teacher and pupil to walk along a river together, a symbolic act meant to impress upon the child that the Torah is like a river, in keeping with Proverbs 5:16: "Let your springs [= teachings] be [like streams] gushing forth." Apparently, after this ceremony, the egg and honey cake, which each child still holds aloft in the illustration, would be eaten.[9]

V. *Bar Mitzvah*

Prior to age thirteen, the male child himself was not expected to perform *mitzvot*, but all *mitzvot*, such as circumcision, donating the *Wimpel* or the *pidyon ha-ben* ritual, had been done either to or for him. At age 13, however, the Jewish youngster commits himself, he literally yokes himself (*'ol torah*), to the system of *mitzvot*. He becomes a *bar mitzvah*, a son of the commandment, bearing his own religious responsibility.

---

[9] E. Roth, "Torah Instruction of Children at Shavuot," *Yeda-'Am*, 11 (1965), 9-12 (Hebrew).

Although the ceremony is very popular in modern times, no trace of it can be found in Jewish sources before the thirteenth century. In the fourteenth century it was widely practiced in the Rhineland. Usually on the first Sabbath after his thirteenth birthday, the boy was called up to the Torah for the first time and read from the Torah scroll to indicate that he had now reached the age of religious and legal majority, could be admitted to membership in the synagogue, and could be counted as a responsible member of the Jewish community. He was now liable for the observance of all the commandments, and to symbolize this transition, at the time the son was called to the Torah, the father recited the following formula: "Blessed be He who has divested (or freed) me of responsibility for [the sins of] this one." [10]

Around the sixteenth century, to have a festive Sabbath afternoon meal became customary, and on occasion the Bar Mitzvah boy would deliver a *derashah*, an appropriate learned discourse to demonstrate his competence in Torah (Plate XIX).

Bar Mitzvah, as a late medieval ceremony, was probably modelled on or influenced by the Christian rite called the *sacrament of adolescence* or *spiritual progress*, which confirmed the baptismal vows of grace (Baptism was considered spiritual birth). Like the Bar Mitzvah, Confirmation marked the recipient's mature acceptance of faith and his admittance to full privileges in the Church. He was now personally responsible for compliance with Confession and Communion.

VI. The Jewish Wedding

Next to Torah study, one of the important *mitzvot* in Judaism is to get married (Genesis 2:24). As a matter of fact, according to Jewish law, a man is obligated to take a wife in order to fulfill the *mitzvah* of propagation. In Ecclesiasticus 26:3 we read: "Happy is the man who has a good wife, the number of his days is doubled." According to the Babylonian Talmud (*Yevamot* 62b) "whosoever spends his days without a wife has no joy, nor blessing, nor good in life." The *Zohar Ḥadash* 4.50b asserts that "the *Shekhinah* (Divine Presence) can rest only upon a married man, because an unmarried man is but half a man, and the *Shekhinah* does not rest upon that which is imperfect."

Though no illustrations or artifacts of marriage from the biblical period have survived, the Bible clearly tells us about wedding feasts (Genesis 24:53, 29:22), the adornment of the bride (Isaiah 49:18, 61:10) and the stipulated payment of a bride's price (Genesis 34:12; Exodus 22:15-16). This bride's price was called *mohar*. It was a sum of money which generally the father of the bridegroom was required to pay the bride's father. Through the *mohar* the bridegroom aquired the right over his future wife, though he could neither buy nor sell her.

During the talmudic period the wedding changed drastically. Now it consisted of two separate and distinct ceremonies. In the betrothal ceremony, known as *kiddushin* (or *ᵓerusin*), the woman was legally married, although she remained in her father's house. The nuptial (or wedding) ceremony, known as *nissuᵓin*, was usually held a year later at the groom's or at his father's house. After the recitation of the nuptial blessings the groom led the bride into the *ḥuppah* (a pavilion or bridal chamber) where the wedding was sexually

---

[10] S. B. Freehof, "Ceremonial Creativity among the Ashkenazim," Gutmann, *Beauty in Holiness*, 493ff.

consummated in strict privacy and the bride passed from her father's authority to her husband's.

Although talmudic sources allude to bridal processions, dances and other wedding celebrations, which flourished in Palestine and Babylonia, and describe the bridal pavilion of ''crimson silk embroidered with gold'' (Babylonian Talmud, *Bava Batra* 146a, *Kiddushin* 50a), we have no visual records of the ceremonies, nor have we any objects in use at that time.

While in the Bible, a wife was acquired by means of the *mohar*, in the talmudic betrothal ceremony she was consecrated, or set apart, from all other women, by her husband to-be. This rabbinic ceremony, called *kiddushin*, required the bridegroom to give to his bride in the presence of two qualified witnesses an object worth no less than a *perutah* (a small copper coin, the *kesef kiddushin*). The bride also received a *shetar kiddushin* (a written contract), called *ketubbah*, which, especially in Palestine, sometimes carried the written formula: ''Be you consecrated to me according to the Law of Moses and the Judaeans.'' Introduced by the rabbis, the *ketubbah* was written in Aramaic, the *lingua franca* of Jews at that time. It was originally a writ of betrothal which served as a legal declaration in writing, signed and witnessed by two witnesses. It signified that the betrothal ceremony (*ʾerusin*) was an act of provisional marriage, and for all practical purposes it bestowed on the bride the status of a married woman.

The *ketubbah* was devised to check the husband's freedom to divorce, as no consent from the wife was required. The contract established the financial and personal obligations the husband assumed for his wife. It protected her social status and property by means of a legally enforceable document in case of the husband's death or divorce. By the geonic period, the text of the *ketubbah* had been standardized in Babylonia. In the text we find that the minimum amount of 200 *zuzim* (silver coins) was the amount of liability set for virgins and 100 *zuzim* for non-virgins (widows or divorcees). This amount could be augmented (*tosefet ketubbah*) by the husband and mentioned in the *ketubbah* or a separate contract. The *ketubbah* also listed the dowry (*nedunyaʾ*) the wife brought with her and the amount the husband contributed of his own free will as the equivalent of her dowry. This was a monetary obligation which the husband agreed to return, if necessary. It also spelled out the ordinary personal obligations of a husband to his wife. With minor textual differences and the description of the dowry and the *tosefet ketubbah* varying from community to community, the prescribed formula is still adhered to in the traditional contemporary *ketubbah*. It reads:

> On the ... (day of the week), the ... day of the Hebrew month of ..., in the year ... thousand, ... hundred and ... since the creation of the world, according to the era which we are accustomed to reckon here in the city of ... (name of city, state and country—in older *ketubbot* the name of the river near the city was sometimes given) ... (name of bridegroom), son of ... (name of father) said to this virgin (or widow or divorcee), ... (daughter of) ... (name of father): ''Be my wife, according to the Law of Moses and Israel, and I will work for, honor, support and maintain you in accordance with the custom of Jewish husbands who work for, honor, support and maintain their wives in truth. And I herewith make a settlement with you, a settlement of virgins, 200 silver *zuzim* (or 100 *zuzim* for widow's and divorcees), which belongs to you, according to the Law of Moses and Israel; and [I will provide you] with food, clothing and necessaries, and will live with you in conjugal relations according to universal custom.''

And ... (name of bride), this virgin (widow or divorcee) consented to become my wife. The dowry which she brought to him from her father's (or family's house), in silver, gold, valuables, wearing apparel, home furnishings, and bedclothes, all this ... (name of bridegroom) accepted in the amount of 100 silver pieces (for widow or divorcee the sum is 50 silver pieces, cf. Deuteronomy 22:29), and ... (name of bridegroom) consented to increase this amount from his own property with the sum of 100 silver pieces making in all 200 silver pieces (in case of a widow or divorcee it was 100 silver pieces). And then said ... (name of bridegroom): "The responsibility of this marriage contract, of the dowry, and the additional sums, I take upon myself and heirs after me, so that they shall be paid from the best part of my property which I now possess or may hereafter acquire. All my property, real and personal, even the mantle on my shoulders, shall be pledged and mortgaged to secure payment of this marriage contract, of the dowry, and of the addition made thereto during my lifetime and after my death, from the present day and forever." ... (name of bridegroom), has taken upon himself the responsibility of this marriage contract, of the dowry and the addition made thereto, as is customary with all marriage contracts and the additions thereto made for the daughters of Israel, in accordance with what our sages of blessed memory established. It is not to be regarded as an illusory obligation or as a simple formal draft. We have followed the legal formality of symbolical delivery (*kinyan*) between ... (name of bridegroom), son of ..., and ... (name of bride), the daughter of ... (name of father), this virgin (or widow or divorcee), and we have used an instrument legally fit for the purpose, to strengthen all that is stated above,
And everything is now valid and binding.
Attested to ... (names of two witnesses).

The earliest illustrated *ketubbot* appear to stem from Islamic Egypt and Syro-Palestine and date roughly from the eleventh and twelfth centuries. These *ketubbah* fragments are from the Cairo Genizah and have yet to be published and studied. Their decorative designs are similar to those found in surviving contemporary Egyptian Islamic marriage contracts (Plate XXa). This practice of illustrating the *ketubbah* was probably adopted in the European Islamic centers of Jewish authority which supplanted the centers in the declining Eastern Islamic world. Unfortunately, there is no surviving evidence of what the decorated *ketubbah* looked like in Islamic Spain. Our evidence comes from thirteenth-fifteenth century Christian Spain where a few ornamented *ketubbot* are extant. These examples again reveal decorated border designs, but are insufficient to render firm conclusions.[11] Rabbi Simeon ben Zemaḥ Duran (1361-1444) of Mallorca, Spain (*Sefer Tashbetz*, responsum 6) tells us that it was customary to embellish borders of the *ketubbot* with decorations and biblical verses so that additional obligations not originally agreed upon could not be inserted in the blank spaces.

In some medieval Islamic Jewish communities during the geonic period the groom simply handed the rolled up *ketubbah* to his bride after the betrothal ceremony and recited the formula: "Behold, here is your *ketubbah* according to the Law of Moses and Israel." That this practice continued in some Italian Jewish communities is apparent from a *maḥzor* miniature from 1481 Pesaro (Plate XXb) where in the presence of two witnesses the groom recites the formula and hands the rolled up *ketubbah* to his bride after the nuptial benedictions. Since these Italian *ketubbot* were generally not read aloud or displayed there was little incentive to decorate them. By the sixteenth century, however, the Jews of Italy had

---

[11] F. Cantera-Burgos, "La 'KETUBA' de D. Davidovitch y las ketubbot españolas," *Sefarad*, 33 (1973), 375-386.

adopted the Ashkenazi custom of reading the *ketubbah* between the combined ʾerusin-
nissuʾin ceremonies and the decorated *ketubbah* came into full bloom among them. The
emergence of the ornamented *ketubbah* in Italy surely owed much to the influx of Sefardim
(Spanish-Portuguese Jews) in the late sixteenth century, who in all probability may have
brought with them the custom of illuminating or decorating the *ketubbah*. The ostentatious
display of the *ketubbah* by wealthy Italian Jews may also have been prompted by a related
non-Jewish practice—public display of majolica plates at the wedding ceremony in
accordance with a well established practice in sixteenth-century Italy. Such plates bear
portraits of the betrothed or allegorical symbols—scenes similar to those found in *ketubbot*.
The custom of decorating *ketubbot* with depictions of bridegroom, bride (Plate XXIa), sun
and moon elicited rabbinic censure. Rabbi Abraham ben Moses di Boton of sixteenth-
century Salonica, Turkey (*Leḥem Rav*, No. 15) and Rabbi Isaac Lampronti of eighteenth-
century Ferrara, Italy condemned this practice, but Jews in Italy and elsewhere generally
ignored such rabbinic exhortations. To curb the insatiable hunger for status by lavish
expenditures on *ketubbot* for public display at Jewish weddings, sumptuary laws
(*pragmatiche*) were enacted by Italian Jewish communal authorities. These *pragmatiche* from
Rome in 1702 and Ancona in 1766 contained a clause limiting the amount of money that
could be expended for the illumination of a *ketubbah*.

The practice of decorating *ketubbot* rapidly spread to Sefardim living in such cities as
Amsterdam (Plate XXVIa), Rotterdam, Hamburg, Gibraltar (Plate XXVIb), and areas
under Venetian domination, such as Corfu (Plate XXIIb). Even rich Ashkenazim there
adopted the custom of having their *ketubbah* illuminated, though elsewhere Ashkenazim
did not adopt the custom of ornamenting *ketubbot* and only one example from late
fourteenth-century Krems, Austria, has come down to us (Plate XXc).

These large rectangular Italian parchment *ketubbot* had their top edges trimmed in a
variety of contours. In Rome, it was customary to trim the bottom edge of the *ketubbah*
(Plate XXIVb). The text of the *ketubbah* was often framed within one or two architectural
portals (Plates XXIb, XXIIb, XXIIIa, XXVa-b)—a practice also found in Jewish and
non-Jewish frontispieces of printed books. Pious sentiments appear in bold Hebrew letters
above the arches, such as "He who finds a wife has found happiness" (Proverbs 18:22)
(Plates XXIIa, XXIVb). Sefardim preferred to place the words *siman tov* (good omen) on
top of the text, while Ashkenazim used *mazzal tov* (good constellation). Many 17th-18th
century marriage contracts combine the words *siman* and *mazzal tov* (or the Aramaic
equivalent) (Plates XXIIb, XXIVa-b, XXVa, XXVIb). Whether the placement of the
words *siman tov* in a panel above the text of the *ketubbah* is an old Sefardi practice is difficult
to establish given the sparcity of evidence. It is, however, found in *ketubbot* from Islamic
Egypt during the twelfth century and thereafter. The *tenaʾim* (written conditions of
additional financial obligations, dowry, etc. mutually agreed upon by the parties concerned, or their families, prior to the wedding) were sometimes set forth in the left hand
column of Italian wedding contracts.[12] It was a very popular custom in Italy to depict a
biblical scene in the Jewish marriage contract. Such a scene usually related to the groom's
Hebrew name (Plate XXIIa-b) or, in isolated cases, to the name of the bride. This
practice began in 17th-century Italy and can be linked with the contemporary Sefardi

---

[12] In Ashkenazi regions, a separate contract containing the *tenaʾim* was customary.

practice, especially in Holland, of placing biblical scenes relating to the Hebrew first names of the deceased on marble tombstones (Plate XLV). A *ketubbah* from Ferrara, Italy in 1775, shows two women standing on plinths and supporting an architrave crested by the prophet Samuel, who is flanked by Moses holding the tablets, and Aaron with a censer. Underneath the prophet is the inscription: "And Samuel grew and the Lord was with him" (I Samuel 3:19). Hands giving the priestly benediction are placed in a cartouche next to the two figures and an undulating band at Samuel's feet carries the biblical verse from Psalm 99:6: "Moses and Aaron among His priests, Samuel among those who call on His name—when they called the Lord, He answered them." The figure of the prophet Samuel was chosen, no doubt, because one of the names of the bridegroom was Samuel (Plate XXIIa). Similarly, on Corfu in 1781, a contract made for a bridegroom named Joseph depicts the biblical story of Joseph greeting his younger brother Benjamin. The inscription above the figures comes from Genesis 49:22: "Joseph is a fruitful bough, a fruitful bough by a spring; its branches run over a wall" (Plate XXIIb).

Many of the *ketubbot* have symbolic coats-of-arms adopted by rich Jewish Italian families (Plates XXIb, XXIIIb, XXVa). These coats-of-arms followed a practice adopted by newly rich Italian families, but were unlike those of Christian nobles, as they had been neither officially bestowed nor registered. The decorations on the borders of Italian *ketubbot* often included such standard late Renaissance motifs as nude heralds, putti, caryatid female busts and garlands (Plates XXIa-b, XXIIa, XXIIIb, XXVa). Included too, are the 12 zodiacal signs (Plate XXIIIb), as popular belief held that these controlled human destiny. Contemporary allegorical personifications of Justice, Charity, Modesty and Hope as well as mythological figures, like the goddess Venus Urania, the goddess of noble love, are also found (Plates XXIVa-b).[13]

Some Italian *ketubbot* also add an *epithalamium* (a lyric ode written in honor of the bride and bridegroom) placed in the empty space at the bottom of a *ketubbah* or woven into the border designs.[14] In Italy, it was also customary to include Psalm 128 in the marriage rite. Along with imaginary depictions of Jerusalem and its holy buildings (Plate XXIa), we therefore find at times above the *ketubbah* text verses from Psalm 128:5: "May the Lord bless you from Zion. May you share in the prosperity of Jerusalem."[15]

The artists who designed these *ketubbot* are generally not known. In a few cases the names of the artists-scribes—Judah Frances and Elisha of Ascoli (Plate XXIa-b)—are known to us.

Many *ketubbot* are also preserved from Islamic countries, especially from the 19th and 20th centuries—with isolated examples of earlier date (Plates XXa, XXVIIa). Unlike European examples, most of these *ketubbot* are written on paper. These marriage contracts reveal primarily geometric, animal and floral decorations. Their ornamented patterns at

---

[13] S. Sabar, "The Use and Meaning of Christian Motifs in Illustrations of Jewish Wedding Contracts in Italy," *Journal of Jewish Art*, 10 (1984), 47-63. On the general subject, cf. the fine study by S. Sabar, "The Beginnings and Flourishing of Ketubbah Illustration in Italy: A Study in Popular Imagery and Jewish Patronage during the 17th and 18th Centuries," Unpublished Ph.D. dissertation, University of California, Los Angeles, California (in progress).

[14] H. Lazar, "À propos d'une *ketubah* italienne du XVIIe siècle: Réemploi de support et épithalame," *Revue des études juives*, 138 (1979), 367-383.

[15] I. Fishof, " 'Jerusalem above my chief Joy': Depictions of Jerusalem in Italian Ketubot," *Journal of Jewish Art*, 9 (1982), 61-75.

times resemble the intricate ornamentation found on Islamic rugs and on illuminated marriage contracts. Contracts from Isfahan, Persia depict a lion imposed on the rising sun with a human visage—the national symbol of Persia. Local variations from Persian cities like Herat (Plate XXVIIb), Teheran and Meshed, as well as those from cities in Afghanistan, India, Syria, Palestine and Yemen, deserve publication and scholarly investigation.

Just as the *ketubbah* underwent a change from an economic instrument simply handed over to the bride at betrothal in the talmudic period to a contract actually read between the *ʾerusin-nissuʾin* benedictions—due to the fusion of the two separate ceremonies in medieval European communities—so did the *kiddushin* (the betrothal consecration) of the bride by the groom. For the symbolic *perutah* (a small copper coin or its equivalent) given during talmudic times, a gold, unadorned ring (*tabaʿat kiddushin*) was usually substituted. In addition, by the twelfth century, the rabbis in many European Jewish communities had decreed that the groom, while placing the gold ring on his bride's finger, recite orally the now familiar *kiddushin* formula: "Behold you are consecrated to me with this ring according to the Law of Moses and Israel." The groom often placed the ring on the index finger of the bride's right hand in Ashkenazi communities (Plate XXXa, XXXIIIa). In Italy, a separate ring ceremony was instituted in the Middle Ages. This ring ritual might be a part of the wedding service, but it preceded the combined *ʾerusin* and *nissuʾin* ceremonies. The officiant, as many an Italian Hebrew miniature shows, grasped the arms of the couple and gently brought their right hands together. The groom held a ring, which in the process of the union of their hands would be placed on the bride's finger (Plate XXVIIIa-b). Different Italian communities had their own customs as to what hand or finger the ring was to be placed on. This Italian Jewish practice had long non-Jewish antecedents. In artistic depictions from the Roman world, the personification of Concordia sometimes stands between the couple and unites their right hands (*dextrarum iunctio*) as a betrothal symbol of mutual trust. At times the bride also received a ring which she slipped on her index finger (*anulus pronubus*). In the Roman Catholic church, the ring was also employed, and the officiant often linked the couple's right hands with the declaration that he was joining them to the hands of the Lord.

Although we have many artistic images of the marriage ceremony from the thirteenth century on, we have no rings that definitely can be assigned to this early period. Rings with precious stones are at times described in Jewish literature and eighteenth century sources mention that the words *mazzal tov* are sometimes engraved on the wedding rings. Still, the elaborate gold rings with gold filigree and enamel ornamentation, often topped by an elaborate building, are an enigma. These rings have been attributed to Venice, Northern Italy and Southern Germany by many scholars and dated from the sixteenth to the eighteenth centuries (Plate XXIXb-d). These ornate rings were reputedly used only during the actual wedding ceremony, but remained the property of the synagogue. The buildings atop these rings have received several contradictory interpretations. According to scholarly opinion, they symbolize the new home of the couple, the synagogue, or the Temple of Jerusalem. Israel Abrahams dismissed them by stating that they are not "rings at all ... but ... [bridal] bouquet holders."[16] These rings, which make their appearance in

---

[16] I. Abrahams, *Jewish Life in the Middle Ages* (New York, 1958), 181.

various collections and catalogs in the second half of the nineteenth century, deserve detailed scholarly scrutiny.

The nuptial pavilion or bridal chamber (*huppah*) of the talmudic period was also changed. The combined betrothal-wedding ceremony was not only shifted from the home to the synagogue, but the *huppah* now consisted of spreading or covering the bridal couple with a cloth (*sudar* = *sudarium*) or a *tallit* (prayer shawl), or the cowl of the groom's garment was stretched over the bride (Plates XXIXa, XXXa-b). A similar practice existed in the Catholic Church, where, during the nuptial Mass, a cloth (*pallium, velamen, velum*) was sometimes spread over the bridal couple. This latter custom was explained by reference to such biblical statements as ''Spread your robe over your handmaiden'' (Ruth 3:9) or ''I spread My robe over you'' (Ezekiel 16:8).

From the sixteenth century on, it became customary in Ashkenazi lands to hold the wedding in the courtyard of the synagogue. The *huppah* was now a portable canopy, its four poles sometimes upheld by four boys, and the bride and groom were now led under the *huppah* and not into it as in talmudic times (Plates XIIa, XIIIa-b, XXXIa, XXXIIIa). The fabric stretched over the staves could be a *parokhet* (Torah ark curtain) or a cloth, at times blue to suggest heaven. The cloth itself often had a Hebrew inscription and depictions of sun, moon, and stars so that it might resemble the heavens and be an omen that the couple's children ''shall be as numerous as the stars of heaven'' (Genesis 22:17). A portable canopy called *mappula* or *Traghimmel* was employed earlier in Catholic church ritual, and it was probably adapted by Jews from Catholicism. In some of the wedding illustrations both the portable canopy and the spread *tallit* were employed (Plate XXXIIIa).

By the eighteenth century, it had also become common to employ silver wedding cups for the two required blessings over wine. They consisted at times of two matched cups which fitted together to resemble a coopered barrel. Sometimes they were inscribed with appropriate Hebrew verses from the wedding service. During the late Middle Ages, it was customary to use a wine flask with a narrow opening (called *Gutterolf*) to signify that the bride was a virgin (Plate XXXIIIa). For a non-virgin, a wine flask (called *Krause*) with a wide opening was employed. In talmudic times, it was customary to roll a closed cask of wine before a virgin during the wedding procession and an open one before a non-virgin (Babylonian Talmud, *Ketubbot* 16b). A glass cup over which the wedding blessings had been recited was also thrown at a stone, affixed usually to the northern wall of the Ashkenazi synagogue; the stone had the shape of a carved octagonal or hexagonal star, variously called *sigillum Salomonis* (seal of Solomon) or *scutum Davidis* (shield of David). [Later, in many Ashkenazi communities, the glass over which the betrothal benediction had been recited would be hurled at the stone—nowadays, a separate glass vessel is broken.] These medieval carved stones were also known as *huppah* stones, stars, or *Traustein*, and they sometimes had the initial Hebrew letters of Jeremiah 7:34 carved on them: ''the sound of mirth and gladness, the voice of bridegroom and bride.'' (Plate XXXIa-b). The rabbis, unable to abolish this popular custom, tried to justify it by claiming that it served as a reminder of the destruction of the Jerusalem Temple (*zekher lahurban*). The practice probably arose because of the folk belief that evil forces resided in the northern regions and that the harm they might inflict on the couple could be warded off. Thus the glass cup still full of wine was intended as a bribe for the demons. It was also hoped that the broken pieces of glass would injure the demons or that the noise of the shattering glass would frighten them.[17]

The custom was unknown to medieval Sefardi Jews. By the eighteenth century, however, after their expulsion from Spain and Portugal, breaking a glass cup at weddings had become a well-established custom in such Sefardi centers as Holland and England. The glass cup was not cast against the wall and the *huppah* was not set up in the courtyard of the synagogue, as was customary in Ashkenazi communities. In Holland and England, the curtained canopy is at times affixed to the wall of a room or is suspended from the ceiling. An empty glass cup is shattered by throwing it against a silver platter placed at the groom's feet (Plate XXXIIa-b). In Italy, an empty glass cup was thrown on the ground and Leone da Modena in his *Riti ebraici* informs us that the custom was a reminder of the fragility of life, "a recollection of death which can break and shatter us like a glass vessel which cannot be repaired."

As the two separate talmudic ceremonies—ʾerusin and nissuʾin—had been combined in medieval Europe, new engagement ceremonies (known as *shiddukhin*) arose. A *shadkhan* (professional matchmaker or marriage broker) was, from the medieval period on, sometimes engaged to effectuate marriages. This engagement ceremony, known as *Knassmahl* (penalty feast) in Ashkenazi territories, was essentially an engagement party held after the conditions (*tenaʾim*) of the forthcoming match had been agreed upon by the parents of the bride and groom or their representatives and written out in a formal contract. A monetary fine (*kenas*) was stipulated in case of a breach of promise of the engagement by one of the parties. An important aspect of the engagement was the breaking of an earthen vessel to symbolize the certainty that, just as this broken pot can never be put together, so is a broken engagement irreparable (Plate XXXIV).

An important custom observed in medieval Germany was the exchange of gifts (*sivlonot*) between bride and groom, sometimes on the evening prior to the wedding. These gifts were delivered by the rabbi or another official of the community. Among the gifts exchanged were special belts. The belt sent to the groom sometimes had silver clasps, while the one sent to the bride had golden clasps, though a 1716 ordinance from Frankfurt-am-Main tried to prohibit the latter practice. These belts (*Siwlonesgürtel*) adorned the waists of bride and groom during the wedding ceremony (Plate XXXIIIa-b).

Another popular gift was a prayer book with lavish silver binding—a *pragmatica* (sumptuary law) from Rome tried to forbid this fashion in 1726. On occasion the bride would also send a beautiful *tallit* to the groom.

In Ashkenazi regions, it was customary to donate embroidered Torah ark curtains to the synagogue to commemorate this important event, while in Italy embroidered Torah binders were sometimes given.[18]

On the wedding day, both bride and groom were accompanied to the synagogue in festive torch-lit processions. Prior to the wedding, the rabbi or the groom, or both together, ceremoniously covered the bride's face with a veil (*Bedecktuch, henumaʾ* or *hinumah*) on a special *Bedeckstuhl* (chair or sofa) (Plates XXXIa, XXXIIIa). Tradition

---

[17] J. Z. Lauterbach, "The Ceremony of Breaking a Glass at Weddings," *Beauty in Holiness*, ed. Gutmann, 340-369.

[18] J. Gutmann, *The Jewish Sanctuary* (Leiden, 1983), 7.

interpreted this custom as reminiscent of Rebecca who, according to Genesis 24:65, "took her veil and covered herself" when she first beheld Isaac. Covering the bride symbolized that she could no longer look at another man; it was also intended to avoid the evil eye or deceive the demons into thinking that the bride was in mourning. In medieval Germany, the groom put ashes on his head as both a symbol of mourning and a means of deceiving evil spirits.

Bridal crowns or myrtle, olive or flower wreaths were at times worn during the ceremony in the talmudic period as well as in the Middle Ages (Plates XXc, XXXa).

In addition to music (Plates XXXa, XXXIIIa), the merry festivities were enlivened by the employment of a jester (*badḥan*, *letz* or *marshallik*) (Plate XXXIIIa).

VII. The *Ḥalitzah* Ceremony

Jewish law obligates a brother of the deceased to marry a childless widow (Deuteronomy 25:5-6). If the brother refuses to undergo the levirate marriage, then "the [deceased] brother's widow shall go up to him in the presence of the elders, pull the sandal off his foot and spit in his face" (Deuteronomy 25:7-10). This humiliating ceremony of *ḥalitzah*—the act of untying the sandal or shoe of the husband's brother by the childless widow—is the act of renunciation by which the childless widow is released (Plates XXXV-XXXVI).

VIII. Divorce

Although divorce in traditional Judaism is the man's prerogative, tradition frowns upon it, for "if a man divorces his first wife, even the altar (of the Jerusalem Temple) sheds tears" (Babylonian Talmud, *Gittin* 90b). The written bill of divorcement, called the *get*, is unadorned. The *get* is written in Aramaic and must be delivered by the husband to his wife in the presence of two witnesses. After the wife receives the *get*, she returns it to the rabbinical court (*bet din*). The court tears or cuts it so that it may not be used again and to avoid any suspicion that it was not legal. The *get* is then filed away in its torn state.

IX. Death and Burial

As *berit milah* marks the individual male Jew's initiation into the *mitzvah* system, so does death mark its end. To symbolize this fact one of the *tzitzit* (corner fringes) of the *tallit*, with which the deceased is buried, is removed to render it unfit for the performance of *mitzvot*.

The Hebrew Bible places little emphasis on death or the hereafter. Various references speak only of the dead going down to a shadowy existence in *Sheʾol* (a nether world, cf. Genesis 37:35, Deuteronomy 32:22, I Samuel 2:6, Ezekiel 32:27). Life was considered precious and was intended to be lived to the fullest. After the destruction of the Jerusalem Temple in 70 C.E. and during the Middle Ages, the rabbis shifted the biblical emphasis on this world to the other-worldly realm. Through the performance of daily *mitzvot* a Jew could earn a place in *Gan Eden* (paradise = heaven); failure to heed the *mitzvot* would result in condemnation to the tortures of *Gehinnom* (Gehenna = hell). The rabbis stressed the *ʿolam habaʾ* or *ʿatid lavoʾ* (the world, or future, to come) with its promised salvation of every righteous individual soul. According to *Pirkei Avot* 4:16: "This world is like a corridor leading to the world to come: prepare yourself in the corridor that you may enter into the banqueting hall." The soul of every righteous Jew awaited the resurrection when his soul would be rejoined to his resurrected body (*tehiyyat ha-metim*) and would witness the ultimate return to Jerusalem in messianic times (*yemot ha-mashiah*). The feet of the dead were usually placed facing east towards Jerusalem; in Ashkenazi lands a sachet of redemptive soil from the Holy Land was placed under the deceased's head to help expiate his sins for having lived and died in an unclean land and to ensure resurrection in the clean Land of Israel. In addition, at times a shovel or fork was placed next to the deceased to aid him in his progress through underground tunnels (*gulgelet ha-met*) to the Mount of Olives in Jerusalem, where the resurrection of the dead was to take place in the messianic future.[19]

One of the highest *mitzvot* was to take care of the dead. For that purpose, burial brotherhoods came into being. (Women had their own burial societies which looked after the needs of deceased women, cf. Plate XLVIIa.) These burial societies have a long history, but it is only from the sixteenth century that we have records of organized, voluntary, charitable burial societies (variously called *hevrah kaddisha*, *hevrah kaddisha* *gemilut hasadim tovim* or *hevrah kaddisha* *gomelei hasadim*). The regulations (*takanot*) governing its membership were recorded in *pinkasim* (ledgers). The job of the *hevrah kaddisha* was to attend to the needs of the sick and dying and to prepare the corpse for burial, see to the reverential disposal of the dead, and conduct the burial in accordance with traditional Jewish burial practices.

Prior to death, the *viddui* (confessions of sins) of the dying person is heard and often after the departure of the soul there is a recitation of the *tzidduk ha-din* (the justification of the Judgment) prayer affirming faith and acceptance of the death (Plate XXXVIIa). The body is placed on the ground, often strewn with straw, directly after death and is surrounded with lit candles. The body is then taken without much delay to the mortuary, where the burial society members wash the body with warm water, at times mixed with beaten egg, to remove all impurities (*taharah*) and at the same time drive away evil spirits believed to shun water and light (Plate XXXVIIIa). Special silver combs and nail cleaners are used for this purpose (Plate XXXVIIIb). Then the body is dressed in a *Kittel* (also called *sargenes* or *takhrikhin*)—the traditional white linen burial shrouds (Plate XXXVIIb). These shrouds must have no knots; even the threads are unknotted. The color white was chosen, as that is the traditional color associated with angels, who are pure, free of sin. The white shroud may be the selfsame garment that the deceased wore during the two *Seder* (Passover eve) ceremonies, as well as on *Yom Kippur* (the Day of Atonement); *Hasidim* in Poland also wore it at their wedding.

At the cemetery (called *bet ʿolam*, *bet ha-hayyim*, or *bet ha-kevarot*) a *hesped* (eulogy in praise of the deceased) is given and the body is lowered into the grave (Plates XXXIX, XLIIIa). *Hevrah kaddisha* members pass among the throng assembled at the funeral carrying *tzedakah* (alms) boxes and calling out: "Righteousness saves from death" (Proverbs 11:4) (Plates XXXIX, XL).

Usually, a plain, wooden box was used in Europe; in other Jewish communities the corpse would be placed directly into the grave (Plate XLIIIa). The coffins of the righteous

---

[19] J. Gutmann, "Wenn das Reich Gottes kommt: Messianische Themen in der jüdischen Kunst des Mittelalters," *Wenn der Messias kommt*, eds. L. Kötzsche, P. von der Osten-Sacken (Berlin, 1984), 19-26.

and learned Jews sometimes were fashioned from the boards of the table at which the deceased had studied, given meals to the indigent or bestowed generosity or help on the needy. Different stone markers and burial sites have been used throughout Jewish history. The Bible speaks of grave markers (*matzevah* or *tziyyun*, cf. Genesis 35:20, II Kings 23:17 and Ezekiel 39:15). Under Greco-Roman influence, it became customary, especially in Palestine from the first century C.E. on, to rebury the dead after the corpse had been reduced to mere bones. The first burial in a tomb was only temporary. It may have served as a means of atonement for the soul to help it attain expiation and purification through decomposition of the body. After a period of time had elapsed, the second burial took place. The Talmud calls this second burial *likkut ʿatzamot* (the gathering of the bones). The bones were gathered and placed in special receptacles called ossuaries. Often made of white limestone, they were decorated with rosettes, colonnades, palm branches and geometric designs.[20] Very wealthy families might use free-standing sepulchres, veritable houses of the dead. Such an elaborate rock-hewn structure was known as *nefesh* (= house for the soul); some are still extant in the Kidron Valley at Jerusalem.

Somewhat later, especially in the third and fourth centuries C.E., Jews followed the Roman practice of burying their dead in catacombs; the most extensive have been found in Rome and at Beth Sheʿarim in Israel. Poor Jews were placed in *kokhim* (*loculi* = niches) cut into the walls of the catacombs and frequently sealed with a stone bearing a simple Greek or Latin (seldom Hebrew) inscription and Jewish symbols (Plate XLIIa).

Richer Jews had their bodies placed in elaborate sarcophagi, at times sculpted with pagan personifications and scenes drawn from Greco-Roman mythology; these sarcophagi were set in *cubiculi* (burial chambers) of the catacombs (Plates XLI, XLIIb). The *cubiculi* had painted decorations which, apart from such Jewish symbols as the *menorah*, Torah shrine and *shofar*, are indistinguishable in style from *cubiculi* in Roman and Christian catacombs (Plate XLIIb).

Most interesting are tombstones found in Sefardi cemeteries of Ouderkerk on the Amstel in the Netherlands and Curaçao in the Netherlands Antilles. Made of marble or native stone, they carry biblical scenes dealing with the lives of the patriarchs, matriarchs, prophets, kings of ancient Israel and famous biblical heroes and heroines. Thus we find, for instance, the Sacrifice of Isaac, the Judgment of Solomon and Rachel dying in childbirth. These depictions refer to the assumed Hebrew first names of the deceased, who often were former New Christians (so-called Conversos, Marranos or Iberian Catholics) (Plates XLIV-XLV). Frequently commissioned during the lifetime of the interred, these gravestones were made for wealthy and influential Sefardi merchants and diplomats. They proudly carry the armorials of these former Spanish and Portuguese grandees and openly reaffirm and proclaim Jewish ancestral ties. They differ entirely from the austere tombstones of their Dutch Protestant neighbors and from those of their European Ashkenazi brethren. Such elaborately sculpted horizontal Jewish tombstones were unknown even in medieval Spain. Devoid of figural ornamentation, the medieval Spanish Jewish tombstones followed the practice found in Muslim cemeteries.

The Sefardi tombstone inscriptions are primarily Portuguese and Hebrew and date from the seventeenth and eighteenth centuries. The sources of inspiration for these unique

---

[20] P. Figueras, *Decorated Jewish Ossuaries* (Leiden, 1983).

Dutch Jewish tombstones were biblical scenes found in contemporary printed Christian Bibles and Bible histories.[21]

Ashkenazi cemeteries often display sandstone slabs placed in a vertical or upright position (Plate XLIIIa-b). They usually bear simple Hebrew epithets and sometimes symbolic allusions to family names (a goose for the family name Gans, or a bear for the family name Bär), to family occupations or trades (a mortar with pessel for a druggist; scissors for a tailor; a knife for a *mohel*), or to Jewish ancestral descent (hands spread in benediction symbolizing priestly lineage; a hand pouring water from a pitcher alluding to levitical descent). Prominent Ashkenazi Jewish members might have stone tombs resembling small houses with pitched roofs (called ʿohel or *Häuslech*).

Following burial, and in some communities before burial, the symbolic rending (*keriʿah*) of the mourner's garment takes place. The left side of the garment is cut for deceased parents, as this is closest to the heart; for other relatives the right side of the upper garment is cut as a sign of grief. While the garment is cut, the mourner expresses his resignation to God's will by reciting "Blessed be the true Judge." The traditional justification for this custom looks to biblical precedent, Jacob and David rending their clothes in mourning (Genesis 37:34; II Samuel 1:11, 13:31). After the return home from the cemetery, the first meal, known as *seʿudat havraʾah* (meal of comfort), is prepared for the mourners. The mourners then observe *shivʿah* (seven days of strict and deep mourning) by sitting on low stools or on the floor wearing either no shoes at all or shoes without leather. All mirrors are covered, vessels with standing water are poured out in order to drive out the dead spirit that may still be hovering about. Another reason given for the pouring out of water is to prevent the spread of death, since the Angel of Death is held to have cleansed his dripping knife in water. The rabbis derived the seven days of mourning from Genesis 7:4, 10, as they claimed that the Flood was delayed until seven days of mourning for Methuselah had elapsed, and from Job 2:13, where the three friends of Job "sat with him on the ground seven days and seven nights."

The mourning continues for another thirty days, known as *sheloshim*, and such pleasures of life as listening to music, dancing, attending parties, and cutting hair and nails are strictly forbidden. The thirty days of mourning are derived from Deuteronomy 34:8, because "the Israelites bewailed Moses in the steppes of Moab for thirty days."

An Aramaic prayer, called the mourner's *kaddish*, is recited in the synagogue by mourning sons for their parents for a period of eleven months—a span of time deemed sufficient to help the dead souls escape punishment in Gehenna and as proof of religious merit rewarded by happiness in *Gan Eden* (heaven) (Plate XLVI). The *kaddish* prayer, now popularly thought of as a prayer for the dead, is in reality a doxology whose content reveals no link with death or praying for the dead. The custom of reciting a memorial prayer was predicated on the fact that the living could help atone for the sins of the parents and redeem them from *gehinnom*. This custom originated in medieval Christian Europe and was well established in Ashkenazi communities by the thirteenth century. The practice of reciting the mourner's *kaddish* for eleven months as well as of reciting the mourner's *kaddish* on the anniversary of the death of the departed (*Jahrzeit*) and lighting a

---

[21] Cf. R. Weinstein's excellent "Sepulchral Monuments of the Jews of Amsterdam in the Seventeenth and Eighteenth Centuries," Unpublished Ph.D. dissertation, New York University, 1979.

memorial candle (*Jahrzeitlicht*) dates in Ashkenazi territories from the late Middle Ages. These customs reveal the Jewish involvement with Catholic German society and testify to the complex interrelationship of Ashkenazi Jews with their medieval German Christian neighbors.[22]

Once a year the holy burial society fasted, usually on the 7th of *Adar* (others on the 15th of *Kislev*), a day which rabbinic tradition associated with Moses' death (Babylonian Talmud, *Megillah* 13b; *Kiddushin* 38a). The fast ended with a festive banquet. On that occasion *gabba'im* (officers) were elected and new members inducted; all drank from a special silver beaker or had wine poured from it into their cup. Frequently the names of all the members were engraved on the beaker. At times, they also used large splendid silver pitchers and poured the wine into the individual cups. In Bohemia-Moravia, it was customary to have enameled or painted glass beakers and pitchers with scenes of the society's functions and appropriate pious inscriptions. These cups resembled Christian guild goblets[23] (Plates LXVII-LXVIII).

Death, however, is not the end of *mitzvot* or the Jewish life cycle. Those who remain behind praise God daily for His wisdom both in giving life and in taking it away. Although the performance of *mitzvot* by the deceased has ended, it is the obligation of the bereaved to carry on with the *mitzvot* so that, like the perpetually turning wheel, the performance of the cycle of *mitzvot* is ever renewed and unceasing.

---

[22] Gutmann, "Christian Influences on Jewish Customs," 133-138.

[23] I. Shachar, " 'Feast and Rejoice in Brotherly Love': Burial Society Glasses and Jugs from Bohemia and Moravia," *The Israel Museum News*, 9 (1972), 22-51.

CATALOGUE OF ILLUSTRATIONS

Plate I

Ceremonies for the Woman in Labor and Confinement. Nuremberg, 1734. Etching from plate to P. C. Kirchner's *Jüdisches Ceremoniel*. From A. Rubens, *A Jewish Iconography*, London, 1981, p. 55, No. 556. Rubens Collection, London.

Plate II

a) Amulet for the Confinement Room. Germany, early 19th century. Parchment on wood. The corner inscriptions have the names of the angels Semangalof, Shamriel, Sanoi and Sansanoi. The circular inscription is from Psalm 91:7. The inner circle inscription reads: "Adam and Eve, barring Lilith." In the center is the word "Shaddai (Almighty)". A similar tablet is in the Altonaer Museum, Hamburg, No. 29.1.202. Stadtmuseum Köln, *Monumenta Judaica*, ed. K. Schilling, Cologne, 1964, E. 90, fig. 24. Hebrew Union College Skirball Museum, Los Angeles, No. 2.29.

b) Amulet for the Confinement Room. Alsace, early 19th century. Aquarelle on paper. Inscriptions: Psalm 121, "Almighty rend Satan," below the parrot: "Adam and Eve, Abraham and Sarah, Isaac and Rebecca, Jacob and Leah, barring Lilith and her entire entourage, Sanoi, Sansanoi and Semangalof, a witch shall not live..." *Monumenta Judaica*, E 95. Musée Alsacien, Strasbourg, No. 19. Photo: Rheinisches Bildarchiv.

Plate III

a) Circumcision Amulet. Alsace, late 18th century (?). Heart shaped silver filigree container, brocade with piece of paper that has inscription "Shaddai". O. Schnitzler, "Jüdische Beschneidungsamulette aus Süddeutschland, dem Elsass, der Schweiz und aus Hessen," *Schweizerisches Archiv für Volkskunde*, 74 (1978), 41-45. *Monumenta Judaica*, E 43. Musée Alsacien, Strasbourg. Photo: Rheinisches Bildarchiv.

b) *Kreismesser* (Knife to ward off evil spirits). Germany, late 18th century. Iron blade and wooden handle. Inscription on blade: "A witch shall not live." *Monumenta Judaica*, E 97, fig. 28. Musée Alsacien, Strasbourg. Photo: Rheinisches Bildarchiv.

c) Amulet. Italy, 18th century (?). Silver-gilt. Applied Tablets of the Law, menorah, censer, miter and Hebrew inscription "Shaddai." Cf. J. Gutmann, *Jewish Ceremonial Art*, New York, 1968², figs. 51a-b; V. A. Klagsbald, *Jewish Treasures from Paris*, Jerusalem, 1982, p. 89, No. 163. The Jewish Museum, London, *Catalogue*, p. 113, No. 593, plate XLXI.

Plate IV

a) *Gevatter* (Godfather) Awaits the Arrival of the Child. Frankfurt-am-Main, Germany, 1867. Griseille Painting. Artist: Moritz Oppenheim. The scene takes place in the synagogue. The *sandak* is seated, with a cushion on his lap upon which to hold the child for circumcision. In front of him is the *mohel* testing the sharpness of his knife. He is obstructing the empty chair of Elijah. At the door the *Gevatterin* (Godmother) is about to hand the child to the *Gevatter*. A. Werner, *Pictures of Traditional Jewish Family Life*, New York, 1976, p. 23. From Rubens, p. 63, No. 647. Rubens Collection, London.

b) Circumcision Garment and Cover. Germany, 19th century. White silk with silver appliqué. Embroidered inscription: "As he entered into the covenant, so may he be introduced to the study of Torah, *huppah* and good deeds." *Monumenta Judaica*, E 110, fig. 31. The Israel Museum, Jerusalem, No. 165.5A-B. Photo: Rheinisches Bildarchiv.

Plate V

a) Circumcision Bench. Dermbach, Thuringia, Germany, 1767/1768. Wood, painted. Inscription: "Selig Hendel Pach (?)." I. Shachar, *Jewish Tradition in Art. The Feuchtwanger Collection of Judaica*, Jerusalem, 1981, p. 24, No. 9. The Israel Museum, Jerusalem, No. 197.3. Photo: David Harris.

b) Circumcision Chairs. Worms, Germany, 1730/1731. Wood. Inscription: "Donated by Frummet, daughter of Abraham Oppenheim, wife of Aaron Levi" and biblical citations: Ezekiel 10:6ff., Psalm 100:5, Jeremiah 33:11, I Chronicles 16:34, Ecclesiastes 7:14, Genesis 17:8, 10. O. Böcher, "Die Alte Synagoge zu Worms," *Festschrift zur Wiedereinweihung der Alten Synagoge zu Worms*, ed. E. Roth, Frankfurt/Main, 1961, pp. 84, 117-118, fig. 54. Destroyed, formerly in the Jewish Museum of the Rashi Chapel, Worms Synagogue, Worms, Germany.

Plate VI

a) Circumcision Bench. Bischweiler (?), Alsace, ca. 1800. Wood. Inscription from Genesis 17:10: "Such shall be the covenant, which you shall keep", and "This is the Chair of Elijah, may he be remembered for good." *Monumenta Judaica*, E 111, fig. 29. Musée Alsacien, Strasbourg. Photo: Rheinisches Bildarchiv.

b) Circumcision Bench. Rheda, Westphalia, Germany, 1802/1803. Wood. In the cartouche: "Judah Matte (?)." Inscriptions on the right from Leviticus 12:3: "On the eighth day the flesh of his foreskin shall be circumcised," and on the left: "This is the Chair of Elijah, may he be remembered for good." Hebrew Union College Skirball Museum, Los Angeles, No. 15.32.

Plate VII

Circumcision Chair. London, 1826/1827. Mahogany. Inscription: "This is the Chair of Elijah, may he be remembered for good." *Treasures of a London Temple*, ed. L. D. Barnett, London, 1951, p. 65, plate XVI.

Plate VIII

a) Circumcision Cushion Cover. Germany 1731/1732. Linen, embroidered. Within the circle the *sandak* sits on a chair and holds the child on his lap. The *mohel* is in front of him and the mother is at the door. The inscription in the circle reads: "This is for Judah, son of Maharam Stühlingen and his wife, Reikel, daughter of Lengle, Switzerland." Above the scene is the inscription: "This is the Chair of Elijah." Within the outer frame are verses taken from Genesis 21:4: "And when his son Isaac was eight days old, Abraham circumcised him, as God had commanded him." *Monumenta Judaica*, E 106. Schweizerisches Landesmuseum, Zürich, No. LM 4476. Photo: Rheinisches Bildarchiv.

b) Circumcision Cushion Cover. Astrog, Russia (now Poland), ca. 1880. Silk flowered damask with silver thread embroidery. Inscription: "This is the Chair of Elijah, may he be remembered for good." Hebrew Union College Skirball Museum, Los Angeles, No. 1980.126. Photo: Erich Hockley.

Plate IX

Circumcision of the Portuguese Jews. Amsterdam, 1722. Colored Pen Drawing. Artist: Bernard Picart. *Monumenta Judaica*, E 100. Photo: Rheinisches Bildarchiv.

Plate X

a) Circumcision Implements. Amsterdam, 1725. Etching by Bernard Picart. From Rubens, p. 45, No. 451. Rubens Collection, London.

b) Circumcision. North Italy, third quarter of 15th century. Miniature from a manuscript containing Psalms, Job and Proverbs. Biblioteca Palatina, Parma, Ms. Parm. 3596, folio 268v.

Plate XI

a) Circumcision Cups. Augsburg, Germany, 1791-1793. Silver. Master: C. X. Stippeldey. Inscriptions: "Cup of *metzitzah* (suction)" and "Cup of Benediction". The Jewish Museum, London, *Catalogue*, p. 92, Nos. 490, 490a, plate CXLVI.

b) Circumcision Knife. Germany (?), 18th century. Silver handle, embossed with circumcision scene. Similar knives in Bayrisches Nationalmuseum, Munich and Cluny Museum, Paris, No. 12275. *Mitteilungen der Gesellschaft zur Erforschung jüdischer Kunstdenkmäler zu Frankfurt am Main*, III/IV, Frankfurt/Main, 1903, fig. 128; Klagsbald, *Jewish Treasures from Paris*, p. 71, No. 117. Hebrew Union College Skirball Museum, Los Angeles, No. 15.1.

c) Circumcision Knife. Germany, 19th century (?). Agate handle and silver collar. Hebrew Union College Skirball Museum, Los Angeles, No. 15.2.

d) Circumcision Knife. Eastern Europe, 19th century (?). Silver filigree handle. Hebrew Union College Skirball Museum, Los Angeles, No. 15.3.

Plate XII

a) *Torah Wimpel*. Germany, 1731 (Wednesday, 27th Adar II, 5491 = April 4, 1731). Linen, embroidered. In the cartouche at the beginning of the roll: "This was donated by the child Eliakum Gettschlick (?), the son of Joel Kirchhahn from Halberstadt.'' The inscription under the embroidered animals is from *Ethics of the Fathers* 5:20, over the couple standing under the *ḥuppah* are verses from Jeremiah 7:34 and above the Torah scroll with the Ten Commandments are verses from Proverbs 3:18. Gutmann, *Jewish Ceremonial Art*, plate II. Hebrew Union College Skirball Museum, Los Angeles, No. 56.1. Photo: Lelo Carter.

b) *Torah Wimpel*. Bremgarten, Switzerland, 1897 (Tuesday, 23rd Shevat 5657 = January 26, 1897). Linen, painted. Inscription: ''Jacob René Meyer, son of Simḥah ... fecit Guil Silberstein, praeceptor Bremgarten.'' Fenster Gallery of Jewish Art, Tulsa, Oklahoma, No. 74.11.

Plate XIII

a) *Torah Wimpel*. Lower Saxony, Germany, 1795 (Sunday, 14th of Kislev 5556 = Thursday, November 26, 1795?). Linen, painted. Inscription: Ḥayyim, son of Eliezer Segal, son of Simeon Joseph Segal of Imbshausen. Under the word *ḥuppah* is a man holding the prescribed cups of wine, the bride and groom are revealing the ring and the officiant reads from the prayerbook; two musicians are off to the side. *Monumenta Judaica*, E 317, fig. 104; D. Davidovitch, ''Katalog, Tora-Wimpel,'' *Tora-Wimpel*, ed. R. Hagen, Braunschweig, 1978, p. 22, fig. 16. Braunschweigisches Landesmuseum, No. 384d. Photo: Rheinisches Bildarchiv.

b) *Torah Wimpel*. Southern Germany. 1768 (Monday, the 6th of Ḥeshvan 5529 = October 17, 1768). Linen, painted. Under the word *Torah* is an inscription from Proverbs 3:18: ''She is a tree of life to those who grasp her.'' Next to the word *ḥuppah* the rabbi holds the wine cup and the bridal couple display the ring. *Monumenta Judaica*, E 319; Davidovitch, ''Katalog, Tora-Wimpel,'' p. 20, fig. 11. Braunschweigisches Landesmuseum, No. 2811. Photo: Rheinisches Bildarchiv.

Plate XIV

Das Schuletragen (Carrying the son to the synagogue for the presentation of the *Wimpel*). Frankfurt-am-Main, 1869. Griseille Painting. Artist: Moritz Oppenheim. Werner, *Pictures of Traditional Jewish Family Life*, p. 23; J. Gutmann, ''*Die Mappe Schuletragen*: An Unusual Judeo-German Custom,'' *Visible Religion*, 2 (1983), 167. From Rubens, p. 63, No. 648. Rubens Collection, London.

Plate XVa-b

Hollekreisch Ceremony. Southern Germany, 1589. Colored drawings from a liturgical manuscript containing prayers for the Jewish holidays and life cycle ceremonies, written by Eliezer, son of the martyred Mordecai. Below the prayers for the ceremony (Genesis 1:1ff. and Genesis 48:16) two men are depicted lifting the cradle. On the right the mother prepares refreshments. *Monumenta Judaica*, D 44. Germanisches Nationalmuseum, Nürnberg, Germany, No. Hs 7058, folios 43v-44. Photo: Rheinisches Bildarchiv.

Plate XVI

a) Redemption of the First-Born Son. Erlang, 1748. Etching by J. C. Müller to J. C. G. Bodenschatz's *Kirchliche Verfassung*. From Rubens, p. 59, No. 609. Rubens Collection, London.

b) Redemption of the First-Born Son. Amsterdam, 1722. Etching by Bernard Picart. From Rubens, p. 45, No. 453. Rubens Collection, London.

Plate XVII

a) Circumcision Plate (?). Stryj, Galicia, early 19th century. Silver. In the center is the Sacrifice of Isaac and around the rim are the signs of the zodiac. Similar plates are in The Israel Museum, Jerusalem, No. 136.72; The Jewish Museum, New York, No. M 249; Jewish Museum, London, No. 207. Shachar, *Jewish Tradition in Art*, p. 34, No. 52; M. Narkiss, "Jewish Ornamental Plates," *Bezalel Archives* 1 (1928), 105-109. V. Klagsbald Collection, Paris. Photo: Wiemann.

b) Amulet for the Redemption of the First-Born Son. Germany, ca. 1800. Silver. Inscriptions: "Shaddai" and the Hebrew letter "he", which stands for the five *selaᶜim*, the price of redemption. Cf. R. Hallo, *Schriften zur Kunstgeschichte in Kassel*, ed. G. Schweikhart, Kassel, 1983, p. 413, No. 47. Formerly, Hessisches Landesmuseum, Kassel, Germany.

Plate XVIII

Initiation of Jewish Children into the Study of Torah. Southern Germany, ca. 1320. Miniature from a *maḥzor*. *Monumenta Judaica*, D 35; T. and M. Metzger, *Jewish Life in the Middle Ages*, New York, 1982, p. 210, fig. 306; *Machsor Lipsiae*, ed. E. Katz, Leipzig, 1964, pp. 96-97; J. Gutmann, "Shavuot in Art," *The Shavuot Anthology*, ed. P. Goodman, Philadelphia, 1974, pp. 140-141. Universitätsbibliothek, Leipzig, Ms. V 1102/I, folio 131. Photo: Rheinisches Bildarchiv.

Plate XIX

The *Bar Mitzvah* Discourse. Frankfurt-am-Main, Germany, 1874. Griseille Painting. Artist: Moritz Oppenheim. The scene takes place in the home after the synagogal ceremony. Werner, *Pictures of Traditional Jewish Family Life*, pp. 37-39. From Rubens, p. 64, No. 651. Rubens Collection, London.

Plate XX

a) *Ketubbah* Fragment. Egypt, 12th century. Parchment. Cambridge University Library, Cambridge T.S. K 10.14.

b) *Ketubbah* Ceremony in Italy. Pesaro, Italy 1481. Miniature from a *maḥzor*. After the *nissuin* (nuptial) benedictions, the glass is broken and the groom hands the wedding contract to his bride in the presence of two witnesses. He recites the formula: "Behold, here is your *ketubbah* according to the law of Moses and Israel." Hungarian Academy of Sciences, Budapest, Ms. A 390/II, folio 231v.

c) *Ketubbah*. Krems, Austria, 1391/1392 (Friday, ... 5151). Parchment. Groom: Shalom, son of Menaḥem. Bride: Zemaḥ, daughter of Aaron. The bride wears a crown and holds a blue flower; the bridegroom wears the medieval *Judenhut* and holds the ring. K. Schubert, ed., *Judentum im Mittelalter*, Burgenland, 1978, p. 242, No. 18; F. Landsberger, "Illuminated Marriage Contracts," *Beauty in Holiness*, ed. J. Gutmann, New York, 1970, pp. 374-375. Österreichische Nationalbibliothek, Vienna, Cod. hebr. 218.

Plate XXI

a) *Ketubbah*. Carpi, Italy, 1629 (Friday, 12th of Elul 5389 = August 31, 1629). Parchment. Artist-Scribe: Elisha of Ascoli. Groom: Samuel Ḥayyim, son of Abraham Padova. Bride: Eve, daughter of the deceased Raphael Joshua Ravenna. The *ketubbah* text is surrounded by an elaborate outer frame with gilded vine-shoots, plaques and cameos and six roundels with such biblical scenes as Adam and Eve, Abraham and Sarah, Isaac and Rebecca, Jacob and Rachel, Mordecai on horseback and Queen Esther. Jerusalem is depicted in the center of the upper margin. From its midst rises a menorah. In the center of the lower margin are the coat-of-arms of the two families. Inscriptions are drawn from Isaiah, Jeremiah, Psalms, Proverbs and Ruth. The inner, oval border contains gold embellished micrographic verses from Psalm 45, Song of Songs, nuptial songs, etc. In the upper spandrels are two cherubim playing musical instruments and in the lower spandrels are the bride and groom who play the mandolin and viola. L. Grassi, ed., *Italian Ketubbot. Illuminated Jewish Marriage Contracts*, Milan, 1984, pp. 52, 237, plate 3. Biblioteca Estense, Modena, Ms. Or. 85 = αL.2.2 (7).

b) *Ketubbah*. Modena, Italy, 1657 (Friday, 2nd of Nisan 5417 = March 16, 1657). Parchment. Artist: Judah Frances. Groom: Abraham, son of Joseph Finzi. Bride: Laura, daughter of Raphael Rovigo. Two armed guards stand on top of decorated columns, holding spears. The family emblems—a cock and a tree beneath a star and half moon (on the right); a rampant lion facing an ear of corn (on the left)—are held up by two winged figures. Within the wreath is the inscription: "With God's help we will observe and prosper, Amen." The inscription on the plaque held by the two putti at the bottom of the contract is from Genesis 18:18. Landsberger, "Marriage Contracts," pp. 405-406. Hebrew Union College Skirball Museum, Los Angeles, No. 34.66.

Plate XXII

a) *Ketubbah*. Ferrara, Italy, 1775 (Friday, 8th of Adar II, 5535 = March 10, 1775). Parchment. Groom: Arié Samuel Ḥai, son of Moses Ḥayyim ha-Cohen. Bride: Susannah, daughter of Aaron Ḥai ha-Cohen. Two caryatid figures standing on plinths support the architrave crested by the prophet Samuel (alluding to one of the names of the groom), who is flanked by Moses holding the tablets and Aaron with the censer. Underneath the prophet is the inscription: "And Samuel grew up and the Lord was with him" (I Samuel 3:19). Hands giving the priestly blessing are placed in a cartouche next to each of the two figures (as both families are *kohanim* = priests). An undulating band at the feet of Samuel carries the verse from Psalm 99:6. The inscription at the bottom is from

Proverbs 5:18 and that above the *ketubbah* text is from Proverbs 18:22. Gutmann, "Wedding Customs," pp. 319-320. Hebrew Union College Skirball Museum, Los Angeles, No. 34.1.

b) *Ketubbah*. Corfu, Greece, 1781 (Wednesday, 14th of Tishri 5542 = October 3, 1781). Parchment. Groom: Joseph Ḥai Senigallia, son of Judah Senigallia of Ancona. Bride: Diamante, daughter of Jacob Jakur of Corfu. Within the rich floral decoration is a scene of Joseph (alluding to the bridegroom's name) encountering his younger brother Benjamin. The accompanying inscription is from Genesis 49:22. Landsberger, "Marriage Contracts," p. 392. Hebrew Union College Skirball Museum, Los Angeles, No. 34.102.

Plate XXIII

a) *Ketubbah*. Ancona, Italy, 1692 (Wednesday, 8th of Elul 5452 = August 20, 1692). Parchment. Groom: Joseph, son of Immanuel Spiel (?). Bride: Simḥah, daughter of Barukh Zalman. Architectural design of a gate with two bearded figures (probably Moses) pointing to the Ten Commandments held by two winged angels. *Tenaᶜim* below the *ketubbah* text. J. Gutmann, *Jewish Ceremonial Art*, New York, 1968[2], fig. 61; Landsberger, "Marriage Contracts," pp. 393, 412. Hebrew Union College Skirball Museum, Los Angeles, No. 34.109.

b) *Ketubbah*. Conegliano, Italy, 1741 (Friday, 8th of Adar 5501 = February 24, 1741). Parchment. Groom: Shemaryah, son of Samuel Morpurgo. Bride: Bella, daughter of the physician Mordecai Morpurgo. The text is framed with signs of the zodiac and in the corner roundels are such implements of the Temple/Tabernacle as the laver and its stand, the menorah, the ark with cherubim and the table of showbread. Two putti are holding the family crest; the inscription on the band on either side of the crown is from Proverbs 12:4: "A capable wife is the crown of her husband." Many similar contracts of this type are known, cf., for instance, Museo Correr, Venice, No. M. 37197 (Venice, Italy, 1707); Hebrew Union College Skirball Museum, No. 34.62 (Spilimbergo, Italy, 1752); Cluny Museum, Paris, No. 12294 (Modena, Italy, 1755 (?)); Landesmuseum, Kärtner (Gradisco, Italy, 1744). Grassi, *Italian Ketubbot*, plates 11, 13, 16, 21; Landsberger, "Wedding Contracts," p. 397; Klagsbald, *Jewish Treasures*, p. 78, No. 143. K. Schubert, K. Lohrmann, eds., *1000 Jahre Österreichisches Judentum*, Eisenstadt, 1982, Nos. 99 and 99a, figs. 97, 101. Österreichische Nationalbibliothek, Vienna, Cod. Hebr. 136.

Plate XXIV

a) *Ketubbah*. Pisa, Italy, 1790 (Wednesday, 4th of Tammuz 5550 = June 16, 1790). Parchment. Groom: Solomon, son of Raphael De Montel. Bride: Mazzal Tov, daughter of Paltiel Zemaḥ. An allegorical semi-nude figure of Venus Urania and cupid in the top framed panel are surrounded by semi-nudes with bird and dog. Three other semi-nude allegorical figures are in the margins. The *ketubbah* includes the *tenaᶜim*; its top inscription is taken from Jeremiah 7:34. Landsberger, "Marriage Contracts," pp. 400-402; S. Sabar, "The Use and Meaning of Christian Motifs in Illustrations of Jewish Marriage Contracts in Italy," *Journal of Jewish Art*, 10 (1984), pp. 47-48, 55-56. Hebrew Union College Skirball Museum, Los Angeles, No. 34.111.

b) *Ketubbah*. Rome, Italy, 1818 (Monday, 14th of Nisan, 5578 = April 20, 1818). Parchment. Groom: Isaiah Ḥayyim, son of Eliah Toscano. Bride: Hannah, daughter of Judah Joseph Terracini. Inscriptions around the border are from Proverbs 18:22, 128:3, wedding blessings, Ruth 4:11-12. In the upper center panel the bride holds a bouquet of flowers and both bride and groom grasp a heart pierced by an arrow. On the side are such personifications of marriage virtues as *La Bontà* (Goodness nurturing a fledgling that has fallen from its nest), *Amore* (Love—two women embracing) and *La Costanza* (Steadfastness, a woman leaning against a pillar). Landsberger, "Marriage Contracts," pp. 400, 413. Hebrew Union College Skirball Museum, Los Angeles, No. 34.100.

Plate XXV

a) *Ketubbah*. Modena, Italy, 1728 (Friday, 1st of Elul 5488 = August 1, 1728). Parchment. Groom: Shabbetai, son of Isaac Uzziel. Bride: Naomi, daughter of Solomon Foa. A micrographical portal frame is shown with verses from Song of Songs, Ecclesiastes and Ruth. Under the arch are two putti holding a crown—all drawn in micrography. Below the crown and within the micrographical cartouches are the coat-of-arms of the Uzziel (right) and the Foa (left) families. Other biblical inscriptions are from Isaiah, Jeremiah, Psalms and Proverbs. Grassi, *Italian Ketubbot*, 74, plate 14. Biblioteca Estense, Modena, Ms. Or. 86 = αL.2.2 (2).

b) *Ketubbah*. Fiorenzuolo, Italy, 1832 (Friday, 11th of Shevat 5592 = January 13, 1832). Paper cutout. Groom: Zemaḥ, son of Zechariah Mazzal Tov Ottolenghi. Bride: Mazzal Tov, daughter of Abraham Yeḥiel Soave. On top of a palace facade is a mounted figure on horseback (perhaps Napoleon). Below that is a man in a vineyard and a naked woman bathing; a crowned man is looking at her (perhaps David and Bathsheba). The inscription over the arched entranceway is from Jeremiah 23:5. Landsberger, "Marriage Contracts," pp. 382-383, 392, 395. Hebrew Union College Skirball Museum, Los Angeles, No. 34.110.

Plate XXVI

a) *Ketubbah*. Amsterdam, Holland, 1706 (Wednesday, 3d Adar 5466 = February 17, 1706). Paper, copper engraving. Groom: Solomon, son of Isaac Navarro. Bride: Grazia, daughter of Isaac Attias. Flowers are sprouting from large urns. In the upper left corner is a semi-nude woman with two children—an allegory of fertility—and on the right is a contemporary couple. Two cherubs uphold a sheet with the words "with a good sign." The inscription on the bottom left reads: "*27 Adar Seni 5453 Yom Sabat Kodes*" and on the right: "*H. Y. Aboab F.*" (Isaac da Fonseca Aboab was the famous *ḥaham* (= rabbi) of Amsterdam, who had died on Saturday, 27th of Adar II 5453 = April 4, 1693). Landsberger, "Marriage Contracts," pp. 383-384; D. Davidovitch, *The Ketuba*, Tel-Aviv, 1968, pp. 24, 104. Hebrew Union College Skirball Museum, Los Angeles, No. 34.85. Photo: Erich Hockley.

b) *Ketubbah*. Gibraltar, 1902 (Wednesday, 17th of Av 5662 = August 20, 1902). Parchment. Groom: Abraham, son of Samuel, son of Isaac ben Ziḥri. Bride: Clara, daughter of Abraham ben Yunis. A wreath of flowers surrounds the text topped by a large crown (the royal crown of the British Empire, as Gibraltar was a British Crown Colony). The inscription reads: "With a good sign and a favorable constellation and at an acceptable and prosperous time." Gibraltar *ketubbot* usually have the word *ḥai* (= life and the numerical value of 18) in the text and the initials of the bridegroom and bride at the bottom. Davidovitch, *The Ketuba*, pp. 66-67, 95. Hebrew Union College Skirball Museum, Los Angeles, No. 34.202. Photo: Erich Hockley.

Plate XXVII

a) *Ketubbah.* Sanaᶜa, Yemen, 1794 (Friday, 14th of Adar 2105 of the Seleucid era = February 14, 1794). Parchment. Groom: Abraham, son of Mūsá, son of Yaḥyá Salām al-Kohen al-ᶜIrāquī. Bride: Rūmiyah, daughter of Abraham, son of Sālim al-Shaykh al-Levi. Floral border and inscriptions from Jeremiah 7:34, Psalm 40:17, II Chronicles 14:6. The figural decorations are unusual in Islamic Jewish wedding contracts. A. Katz, "A Yemenite Marriage Contract of 1795," *Eretz-Israel*, 6 (1960), 176-178 (Hebrew); *Synagoga*, "Kultgeräte," No. 436. The Israel Museum, Jerusalem, No. 179.8.

b) *Ketubbah.* Herat, Afghanistan, 1895 (Friday, 26th of Av 5655 = August 18, 1895). Paper. Groom: Samuel, son of Isaac. Bride: Michal, daughter of Jacob. Floral decorations around borders; the two miḥrab-like compartments on the top contain verses from Isaiah 61:10. Davidovitch, *The Ketuba*, pp. 76, 100. Hebrew Union College Skirball Museum, Los Angeles, No. 34.204. Photo: Erich Hockley.

Plate XXVIII

a) The Italian *Dextrarum iunctio* and Ring Ceremony. North Italy, third quarter of 15th century. Miniature from a manuscript containing Psalms, Job and Proverbs. Metzger, *Jewish Life in the Middle Ages*, p. 135, fig. 187. Biblioteca Palatina, Parma, Ms. Parm. 3596, folio 275.

b) The Italian *Dextrarum iunctio* and Ring Ceremony. Pesaro, Italy, 1481. Miniature from a *maḥzor*, Italian rite. Hungarian Academy of Sciences, Budapest, Ms. A 380/II, folio 230.

Plate XXIX

a) The Italian Betrothal Ceremony. North Italy, late 15th century. Miniature from a Manual of Jewish Ceremonies (*Hanhagot mikol ha-shanah*). The bride and groom are seated and are covered by a cloth. The officiant holds up the cup of wine to recite the ʾerusin (betrothal) blessing. E. Panofsky, "Giotto and Maimonides in Avignon. The Story of an Illustrated Hebrew Manuscript," *The Journal of the Walters Art Gallery*, 4 (1941), 30. University Library, Princeton, Ms. Garrett 26, folio 17.

b) Wedding Ring. Italy, 17th-18th century (?). Gold and enamel. Inscription around band: "*mazzal tov* (= good fortune)" *Synagoga*, "Kultgeräte," No. 419. Schmuckmuseum Pforzheim, No. 2009.409. Photo: Wiemann.

c) Wedding Ring. Italy, 17th-18th century (?). Gold and enamel. Inscription on roof: "*mazzal tov.*" The Jewish Museum, London, *Catalogue*, p. 84, No. 456.

d) Wedding Ring. Italy, 17th-18th century (?). Gold. The Jewish Museum, London, *Catalogue*, p. 85, plate CXXX.

Plate XXX

a) The Marriage of Moses to Zipporah. South Germany, second half of 15th century. Miniature from the Second Nuremberg Haggadah. The bride wears a crown and the groom is about to place the ring on the index finger of the bride's right hand. The *ḥuppah* is a *sudar* (cloth) spread over the couple. The inscription above the musician reads: "After seven years Moses was freed and wedded the virgin Zipporah." The inscription next to the couple reads: "Behold the betrothal and with a ring they were consecrated." B. Narkiss and G. Sed-Rajna, *Index of Jewish Art*, II/2, Munich, 1981, Card No. 59; Metzger, *Jewish Life in the Middle Ages*, p. 230, fig. 344; Gutmann, "Wedding Customs," p. 314. Schocken Institute for Jewish Studies of the Jewish Theological Seminary of America, Jerusalem, Ms. 24087, folio 12v.

b) Nuptial Ceremony of the German Jews. Amsterdam, 1722. Etching by Bernard Picart. Gutmann, "Wedding Customs," p. 318. From Rubens, p. 45, No. 455. Rubens Collection, London.

Plate XXXI

a) Shattering the Wedding Glass on the *Ḥuppah* Stone of the Fürth Synagogue. Nuremberg, 1734. Etching from plate to Kirchner's *Jüdisches Ceremoniel*. Gutmann, "Wedding Customs," p. 318. From Rubens, p. 54, No. 562. Rubens Collection, London.

b) *Ḥuppah* Stone (or *Traustein*) of the Bingen Synagogue. Bingen am Rhein, Germany, ca. 1700. Red sandstone. Inscription around star is from Jeremiah 7:34. The two cornucopias have the beginning Hebrew letters of Psalm 118:20. *Monumenta Judaica*, E 154. The Israel Museum, Jerusalem, No. 199.22; 1409-9-66. Photo: Rheinisches Bildarchiv.

Plate XXXII

a) Nuptial Ceremony of the Portuguese Jews. Amsterdam, Holland, 1722. Etching by Bernard Picart. Gutmann, "Wedding Customs," p. 318. From Rubens, p. 45, No. 454. Rubens Collection, London.

b) Wedding Plate. Gouda, Holland, ca. 1730. Silver. The glass wedding cup was shattered upon this plate and the congregation shouted *besiman tov* (with a good sign = good fortune) Mikve Israel-Emmanuel Synagogue, Curaçao, Netherlands Antilles. Photo: Fischer.

Plate XXXIII

a) Wedding in the Courtyard of the Old Frankfurt Synagogue. Frankfurt-am-Main, Germany, 1866. Griseille Painting. Artist: Moritz Oppenheim. Bride and bridegroom stand under the portable canopy (*huppah*), whose staves are upheld by four boys. The heads of the couple are covered by a *tallit*. In the foreground, a boy holds a tray with two narrow flasks (called *Gutterolf*) to indicate that the bride is a virgin. While the rabbi recites the blessings, the groom places the ring on the index finger of the bride's right hand. Both wear bridal belts (*sivlonot*) given before the wedding. The *huppah* stone is now a wooden tablet with a *Magen David* (Star of David), which has the words *mazzal tov* in the center and an inscription from Jeremiah 7:34. The *Huppah Schlemiel* or *badhan* (= jester) is on the staircase along with a musician. Werner, *Pictures of Traditional Jewish Family Life*, pp. 41-43. From Rubens, p. 64, No. 652. Rubens Collection, London.

b) Bridal Belt. Frankfurt-am-Main, Germany, third quarter of 17th century. Silver gilt. Master: Peter de Mont. *Monumenta Judaica*, E 176. Gutmann, "Wedding Customs," pp. 316-317. Historisches Museum, Frankfurt-am-Main, No. X 22783. Photo: Rheinisches Bildarchiv.

Plate XXXIV

The Ashkenazi *Knassmahl* (Engagement Party). Nuremberg, 1734. Etching from plate to P. C. Kirchner's *Jüdisches Ceremoniel*. Gutmann, "Wedding Customs," pp. 316, 322. From Rubens, p. 54, No. 559. Rubens Collection, London.

Plate XXXV

a) *Halitzah* Ceremony. Erlang, 1748. Etching from J. C. Müller to J. C. G. Bodenschatz's *Kirchliche Verfassung*. From Rubens, p. 59, No. 615. Rubens Collection, London.

b) *Halitzah* Ceremony. Amsterdam, 1683. Engraving by Jan Luyken to Leo de Modena's *Kerkzeden ende gewoonten ... uit het Italiaans*. Rubens, p. 33, No. 302.

Plate XXXVI

a) *Halitzah* Shoe. Germany, early 19th century. Leather. *Monumenta Judaica*, E 195. The Israel Museum. Jerusalem (on loan from the Kirschner Collection), No. 170.231. Photo: Rheinisches Bildarchiv.

b) *Halitzah* Shoe. Prague, early 19th century. Leather. The State Jewish Museum, Prague, No. 27.325.

Plate XXXVII

a) Prayers at the Deathbed. Prague, ca. 1780. Oil on canvas. D. Altshuler, ed., *The Precious Legacy*, New York, 1983, p. 258, No. 178. The State Jewish Museum, Prague, No. 12.843/2.

b) The Making of the Shroud. Prague, ca. 1780. Oil on canvas. *Precious Legacy*, p. 258, No. 180. The State Jewish Museum, Prague, No. 12.843/4.

Plate XXXVIII

a) The Washing of the Body in the Mortuary. Prague, ca. 1780. Oil on Canvas. *Precious Legacy*, p. 159, No. 181. The State Jewish Museum, Prague, No. 12.843/5.

b) Comb and Nail Cleaners for a Burial Society. Moravia, ca. 1770. Silver. Donor: "Moses, son of Isaac," and an inscription: "A good name is better than fragrant oil, and the day of death than the day of birth (Ecclesiastes 7:1)." *Jewish Art Treasures from Prague*, ed. C. R. Dodwell, Manchester, 1980, p. 142, No. M 130. The State Jewish Museum, Prague, No. 4.520.

Plate XXXIX

a) The Eulogy (*hesped*) over the Dead Man. Prague, ca. 1780. Oil on canvas. *Precious Legacy*, p. 259, No. 185. The State Jewish Museum, Prague, No. 12.843/9.

b) Carrying the Body to the Grave. Prague, ca. 1780. Oil on canvas. *Precious Legacy*, p. 259, No. 186. The State Jewish Museum, Prague, No. 12.843/10.

Plate XL

a) Alms Box. Prerov, 1781. Silver. Inscription: "Donors of the *Hevrah Kaddisha*'—Mordecai, son of Tzevi Hirsch Segal, Leb." *Jewish Art Treasures*, p. 136, No. M 47. The State Jewish Museum, Prague, No. 7.042.

b) Alms Box. Moravia (?), ca. 1819. Silver. Inscriptions: "Donors of the *Hevrah Kaddisha*'—Joshua Ber, son of Aaron; Hayyim, son of Leb Telč Tzalfan; Jacob, son of Solomon Tzoref Pehem (= blacksmith); Nahum, son of Eliakum Glaser." Underneath the clasp is the inscription from Proverbs 10:2: "Righteousness saves from death." *Jewish Art Treasures*, p. 136, M 53. The State Jewish Museum, Prague, No. 3.797.

Plate XLI

Season Sarcophagus. Rome, Via Appia (Vigna Randanini) Catacomb (?), ca. 300. Marble. Winged victories are upholding a *clipeus* with *menorah* and are surrounded by four seasons. K. Weitzmann, ed., *Age of Spirituality*, New York, 1979, pp. 379-380; G. M. A. Hanfmann, *The Season Sarcophagus in Dumbarton Oaks*, Cambridge, Mass., 1951, I, p. 195. Museo Nazionale Romano, Rome, No. 67611.

Plate XLII

a) Tombstone. Rome, Via Appia, late 3rd century or early 4th. Marble. Inscription: "Flavia Dativa set up [this stone] in grateful memory to Flavia Caritina." E. R. Goodenough, *Jewish Symbols in the Greco-Roman Period*, II New York, 1953, p. 23; H. J. Leon, *The Jews of Ancient Rome*, Philadelphia, 1960, p. 298, No. 234. Via Appia Catacomb, Rome. Photo: Rheinisches Bildarchiv.

b) Decorated Arcosolium. Rome, Via Nomentana (Villa Torlonia) Catacomb, late 3rd or early 4th century. Fresco revealing an open Torah ark and Jewish symbols.

Goodenough, *Jewish Symbols*, II, pp. 39-40; Leon, *Jews of Ancient Rome*, plate 25. Via Nomentana Catacomb, Rome. Photo: Rheinisches Bildarchiv.

Plate XLIII

a) Lowering the Body into the Grave. Prague, ca. 1780. Oil on canvas. *Precious Legacy*, p. 259, No. 188. The State Jewish Museum, Prague, No. 12.843/12.

b) Tombstones in the Old Prague Jewish Cemetery. Prague, 15th-18th Century.

Plate XLIV

The Sefardic "Cemetery" at Ouderkerk. Ouderkerk aan de Amstel, ca. 1655. Oil on canvas. Artist: Jacob van Ruisdael. E. Scheyer, "The Iconography of Jacob van Ruisdael's Cemetery," *Bulletin of the Detroit Institute of Arts*, 55 (1977), pp. 133-146. The Detroit Institute of Arts, Detroit, Michigan, No. 26.3.

Plate XLV

a) Tombstones. Amsterdam, 18th century. Marble. Tombstone on the left: Depiction of Ḥaḥam Isaac Aboab da Fonseca in center, flanked by Abraham and David playing his lyre. Inscription: "Ishac Haim Senior, second day of Passover, Nisan 16, 5485 (= April 17, 1726)." Below, the mourning family is shown around the bedside of the dying person. Inscriptions around the border are from Genesis 15:5, Proverbs 4:9, Psalms 38:1, 70:1, 25:15. R. Weinstein, "Sepulchral Monuments of the Jews of Amsterdam in the Seventeenth and Eighteenth Centuries," Unpublished Ph.D. dissertation, New York University, 1979, pp. 391-395. Tombstone on the right: Depiction of Esther petitioning King Ahasuerus (Esther 5:7f.) on top. Inscription: "Ishac (ben Abraham) de Marchena, 7th of Kislev 5491 (= November 16, 1730). Below are scenes of Mordecai on horseback led through the streets by Haman (Esther 6:9f.) and the Sacrifice of Isaac (Genesis 22:12). The scenes of Esther refer to Isaac Senior's wife. Weinstein, pp. 383-385. Cemetery of the Mikve Israel Congregation, Curaçao, Netherlands Antilles. Photo: Fischer.

b) Tombstone. Amsterdam, 18th century. Marble. Depictions of the encounter of David and Abigail (I Samuel 25:20) are on the left and the Judgment of Solomon (I Kings 3:16ff.) is on the right. Inscription: "Abigail (de Daniel Aboab Cardozo) Redondo; Selomoh Nunes Redondo, Sunday, 26th of Tammuz 5515 (= June 18, 1747)." Weinstein, pp. 378-380. Cemetery of the Mikve Israel Congregation, Curaçao, Netherlands Antilles. Photo: Fischer.

Plate XLVI

"Kaddish". Berlin, Germany, 1920's. Oil on canvas. Artist: Joseph Budko. Hebrew Union College Skirball Museum, Los Angeles, No. 41.132.

Plate XLVII

a) Burial Society Beaker. Prague, 1783/1784. Enameled Glass. Inscription: "Cup of Benediction for feasting and rejoicing, drinking one's fill of love. Lovers of survivors, elders stamped in the likeness (?) of the Holy Society of Benefactors, and the new visitors and friends for the care of the sick; for the gathering of the scattered and dispersed. Grace and Unity shall be in His hand to conjoin them, in the year 5544." I. Shachar, " 'Feast and Rejoice in Brotherly Love:' Burial Society Glasses and Jugs in Bohemia and Moravia," *The Israel Museum News*, 9 (1972), pp. 26-27; *Precious Legacy*, p. 254, No. 157.

b) Burial Society Pitcher. Mikulov (Nickolsburg), Moravia, 1836. Painted and gilt pottery. Inscription: "Righteousness saves from death" (Proverbs 10:2, 11:4). "This jug belongs to the Holy Benevolent Society and was made for Mendel Jeitteles, Abraham Isaac Böhm, Moses Leb Bisenz and Ezekiel Maas in the year 5696 (= 1835/1836)." Shachar, pp. 42-43; *Precious Legacy*, p. 255, No. 161. The State Jewish Museum, Prague, No. 8048.

Plate XLVIII

a) Burial Society Beaker. Southern Germany, 1608/1609. Silver, gilt. Master: CM, Frankenthal. Inscription around the rim: "Holy Congregation Worms, 5639." *Monumenta Judaica*, E 210. Museum der Stadt Worms, Worms, Germany. Photo: Rheinisches Bildarchiv.

b) Burial Society Beaker and Cover. Southern Germany, early 18th century. Silver, gilt. Master: Johann Conrad Weiss, Nuremberg (this master fashioned many ceremonial objects for Jewish clients, many of which are still extant). On the handle of the cover is a figure of the rabbi of the district of Ansbach, Bavaria holding a shield engraved with eulogistic references to him and his father. The foot of the beaker shows panels with a bier, a coffin and a gravedigger. Many names of the *Ḥevrah Kaddisha*' of Schwabach, Bavaria are listed as well as other names. The date Sunday, the 11th of Shevat 5470 (= January 12, 1710) is inscribed. Extracts are also incised from Exodus 18:20, and Babylonian Talmud, *Baba Kamma* 99b-100a. The Jewish Museum, London, *Catalogue*, pp. 106-108, No. 570, plate CLIV.

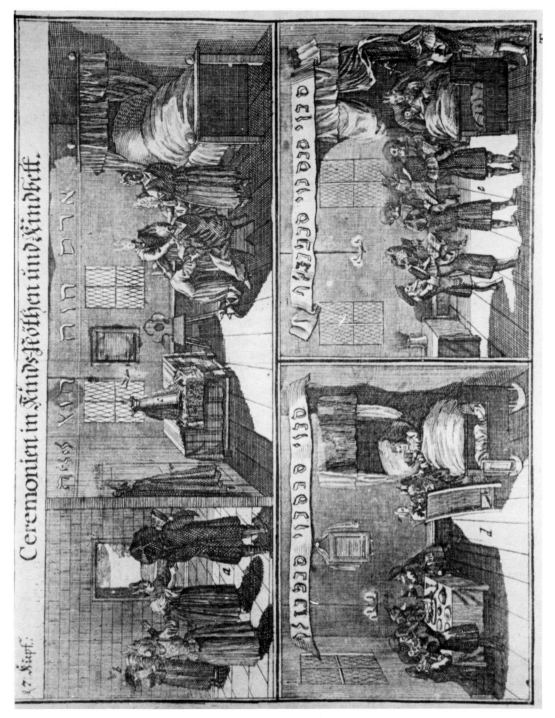

Plate I

Ceremonies for the Woman in Labor and Confinement

Plate II

b) Amulet for the Confinement Room

a) Amulet for the Confinement Room

Plate III

c) *Shaddai Amulet*

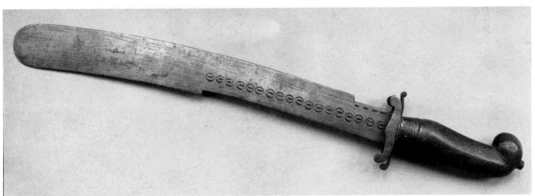

b) *Kreismesser*

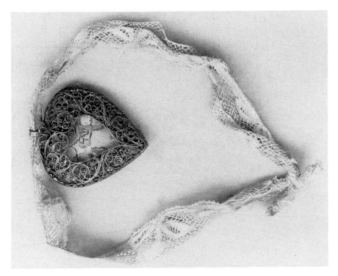

a) Circumcision Amulet

Plate IV

a) The Godfather Awaits the Arrival of the Child

b) Circumcision Garment and Cover

Plate V

a) Circumcision Bench

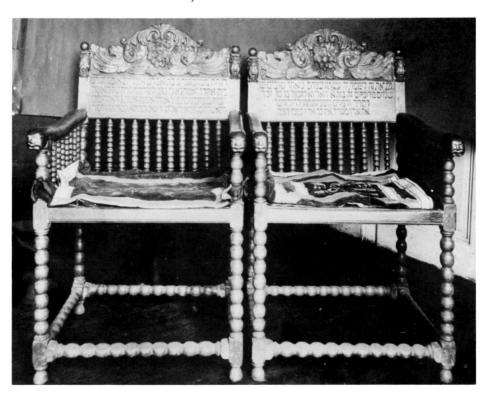

b) Circumcision Chairs

Plate VI

a) Circumcision Bench

b) Circumcision Bench

Plate VII

Circumcision Chair

Plate VIII

a) Circumcision Cushion Cover

b) Circumcision Cushion Cover

Plate IX

Circumcision of the Portuguese Jews

Plate X

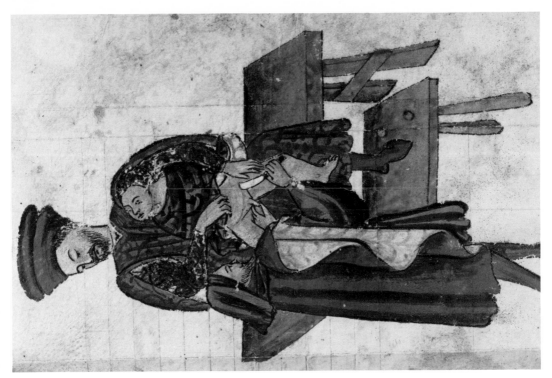

b) Circumcision

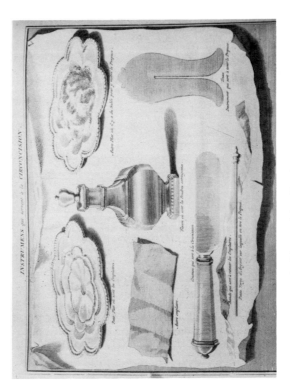

a) Circumcision Implements

Plate XI

a) Circumcision Implements

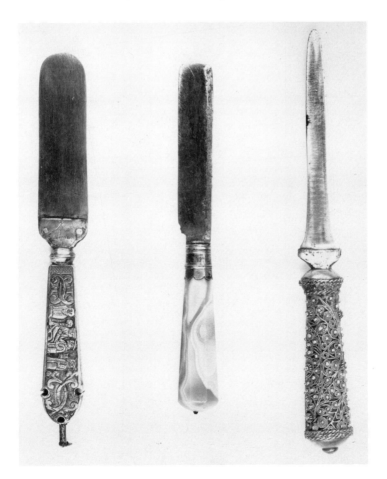

b-d) Circumcision Knives

Plate XII

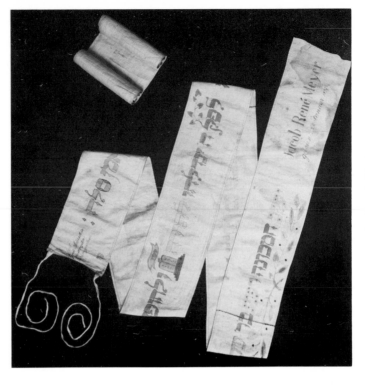

b) Torah Binder

a) Torah Binder

Plate XIII

a) Torah Binder

b) Torah Binder

Plate XIV

Das Schuletragen

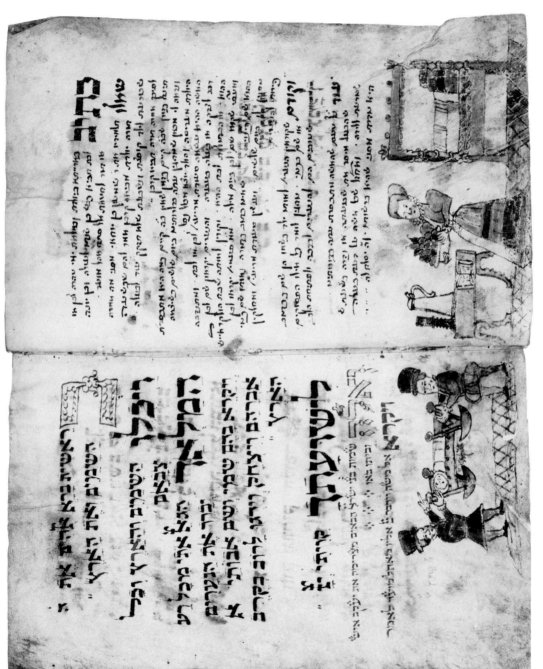

Plate XV

a-b) The *Hollekreisch* Ceremony

Plate XVI

a) The Redemption of the First-Born Son

b) The Redemption of the First-Born Son

Plate XVII

a) Circumcision Plate (?)

b) Amulet for the Redemption of the First-Born
Son

Plate XVIII

The Initiation of Jewish Children into the Study of Torah

Plate XIX

The *Bar Mitzvah* Discourse

Plate XX

c) *Ketubbah*

b) The Italian *Ketubbah* Ceremony

a) *Ketubbah*

Plate XXI

b) *Ketubbah*

a) *Ketubbah*

Plate XXII

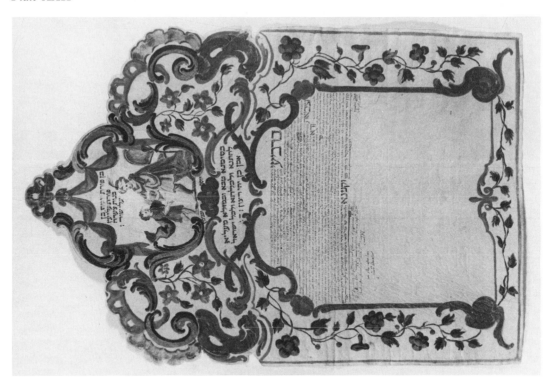

b) *Ketubbah*

a) *Ketubbah*

Plate XXIII

b) Ketubbah

a) Ketubbah

Plate XXIV

b) *Ketubbah*

a) *Ketubbah*

Plate XXV

b) *Ketubbah*

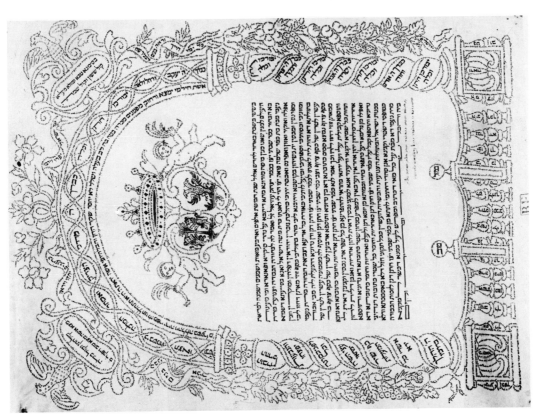

a) *Ketubbah*

Plate XXVI

b) *Ketubbah*

a) *Ketubbah*

Plate XXVII

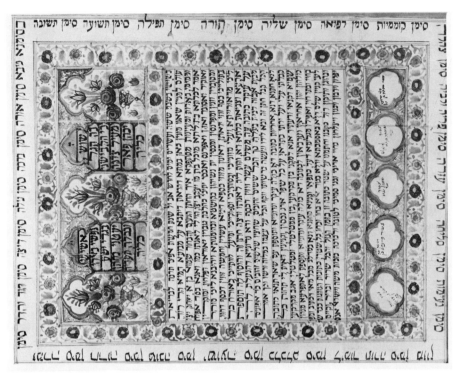

b) Ketubbah

a) Ketubbah

Plate XXVIII

b) The Italian *Dextrarum Iunctio* and Ring Ceremony

a) The Italian *Dextrarum Iunctio* and Ring Ceremony

Plate XXIX

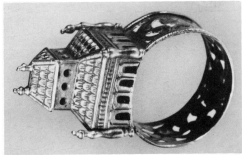

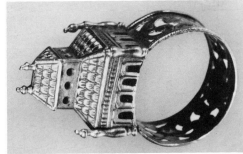

d) Wedding Ring

c) Wedding Ring

b) Wedding Ring

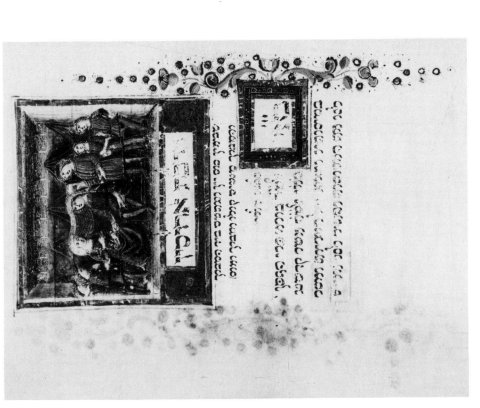

a) Italian Betrothal Ceremony

Plate XXX

a) The Marriage of Moses to Zipporah

b) The Nuptial Ceremony of the German Jews

Plate XXXI

a) The Shattering of the Wedding Cup on the *Traustein*

b) *Traustein*

Plate XXXII

a) The Nuptial Ceremony of the Portuguese Jews

b) Plate for Shattering the Wedding Cup

Plate XXXIII

a) The Wedding in the Courtyard of the Old Frankfurt Synagogue

b) Bridal Belt

Plate XXXIV

The Ashkenazi *Knassmahl* (Engagement Party)

Plate XXXV

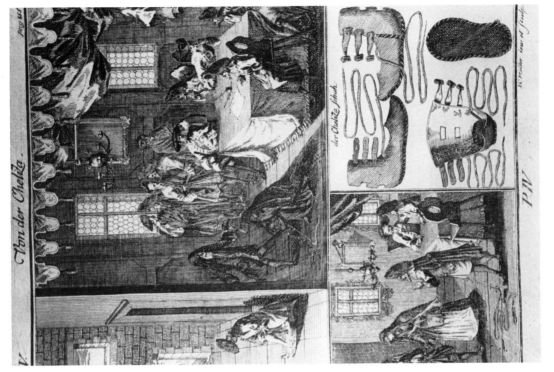

b) The *Ḥalitzah* Ceremony

a) The *Ḥalitzah* Ceremony

Plate XXXVI

a) Ḥalitzah Shoe

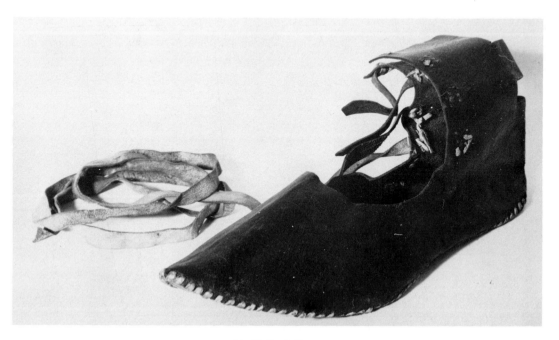

b) Ḥalitzah Shoe

Plate XXXVII

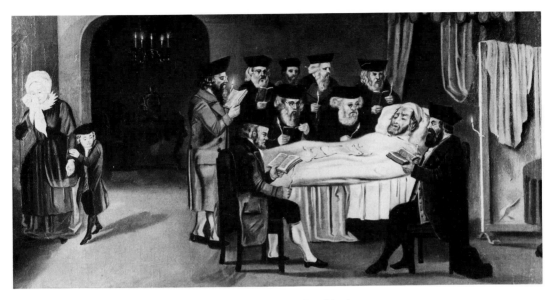

a) Prayers at the Deathbed

b) The Making of the Shroud

Plate XXXVIII

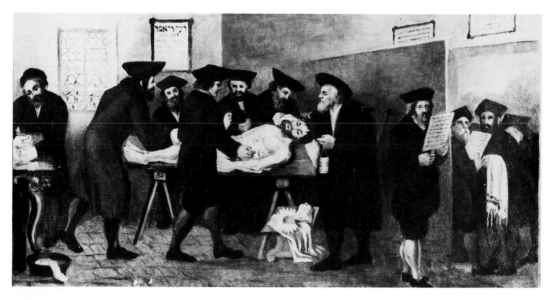

a) The Washing of the Body at the Mortuary

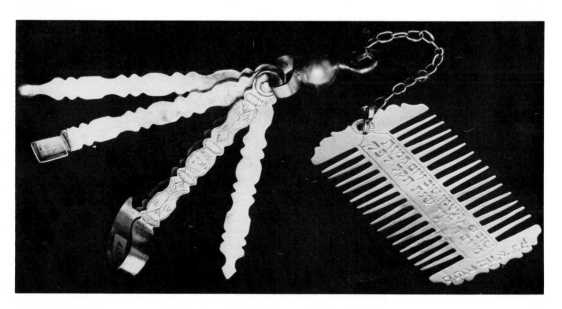

b) Comb and Nail Cleaner of a Burial Society

Plate XXXIX

a) The Eulogy over the Deceased Man

b) The Carrying of the Body to the Grave

Plate XL

b) Alms Box

a) Alms Box

Plate XLI

Season Sarcophagus

Plate XLII

a) Tombstone from the Roman Period

b) Decorated Arcosolium

Plate XLIII

a) The Lowering of the Body into the Grave

b) Tombstones in the Old Prague Jewish Cemetery

Plate XLIV

The Sefardi Cemetery at Ouderkerk

Plate XLV

b) Sefardi Tombstone

a) Sefardi Tombstone

Plate XLVI

"Kaddish"

Plate XLVII

b) Burial Society Pitcher

a) Burial Society Beaker

Plate XLVIII

b) Burial Society Beaker

a) Burial Society Beaker